Impossible Certainty

Cost Risk Analysis for Air Force Systems

Mark V. Arena, Obaid Younossi, Lionel A. Galway, Bernard Fox,
John C. Graser, Jerry M. Sollinger, Felicia Wu, Carolyn Wong

Prepared for the United States Air Force

PROJECT AIR FORCE

The research described in this report was sponsored by the United States Air Force under Contract F49642-01-C-0003. Further information may be obtained from the Strategic Planning Division, Directorate of Plans, Hq USAF.

Library of Congress Cataloging-in-Publication Data

Impossible certainty : cost risk analysis for Air Force systems / Mark V. Arena ... [et al.].
    p. cm.
  Includes bibliographical references.
  "MG-415."
  ISBN 0-8330-3863-X (pbk. : alk. paper)
    1. United States. Air Force—Appropriations and expenditures. 2. United States. Air Force—Costs. 3. United States. Air Force—Cost control. I. Arena, Mark V.

  UG633.2.I6 2006
  358.4'1622—dc22

                                                              2005028332

The RAND Corporation is a nonprofit research organization providing objective analysis and effective solutions that address the challenges facing the public and private sectors around the world. RAND's publications do not necessarily reflect the opinions of its research clients and sponsors.

RAND® is a registered trademark.

Cover design by Stephen Bloodsworth

Published 2006 by the RAND Corporation
1776 Main Street, P.O. Box 2138, Santa Monica, CA 90407-2138
1200 South Hayes Street, Arlington, VA 22202-5050
4570 Fifth Avenue, Suite 600, Pittsburgh, PA 15213
RAND URL: http://www.rand.org/
To order RAND documents or to obtain additional information, contact
Distribution Services: Telephone: (310) 451-7002;
Fax: (310) 451-6915; Email: order@rand.org

Preface

This report is one of a series from a RAND Project AIR FORCE project, "The Cost of Future Military Aircraft: Historical Cost Estimating Relationships and Cost Reduction Initiatives." The purpose of the project is to improve the tools used to estimate the costs of future weapon systems. It focuses on how recent technical, management, and government policy changes affect cost. This report examines cost estimating risk analysis methods and recommends a policy prescription.

The project was conducted within the RAND Project AIR FORCE Resource Management Program. The research is sponsored by the Principal Deputy, Office of the Assistant Secretary of the Air Force (Acquisition), Lt Gen John D.W. Corley. The project technical monitor is Jay Jordan, Technical Director of the Air Force Cost Analysis Agency.

This report should interest government cost analysts, the military acquisition communities, and those concerned with current and future acquisition policies.

Other RAND Project AIR FORCE reports that address military aircraft cost estimating issues include the following:

- In *An Overview of Acquisition Reform Cost Savings Estimates*, MR-1329-AF, 2001, Mark Lorell and John C. Graser use relevant literature and interviews to determine whether estimates of the efficacy of acquisition reform measures are robust enough to be of predictive value.

- In *Military Airframe Acquisition Costs: The Effects of Lean Manufacturing*, MR-1325-AF, 2001, Cynthia R. Cook and John C. Graser examine the package of new tools and techniques known as "lean production" to determine whether it would enable aircraft manufacturers to produce new weapon systems at costs below those predicted by historical cost estimating models.

- In *Military Airframe Costs: The Effects of Advanced Materials and Manufacturing Processes*, MR-1370-AF, 2001, Obaid Younossi, Michael Kennedy, and John C. Graser examine cost estimating methodologies and focus on military airframe materials and manufacturing processes. This report provides cost estimators with factors useful in adjusting and creating estimates based on parametric cost estimating methods.

- In *Military Jet Engine Acquisition: Technology Basics and Cost-Estimating Methodology*, MR-1596-AF, 2002, Obaid Younossi, Mark V. Arena, Richard M. Moore, Mark Lorell, Joanna Mason, and John C. Graser introduce a new methodology for estimating military jet engine costs and discuss the technical parameters that derive the engine development schedule, development cost, and production costs. They also present quantitative analysis of historical data on engine development schedule and cost.

- In *Test and Evaluation Trends and Costs in Aircraft and Guided Weapons*, MG-109-AF, 2004, Bernard Fox, Michael Boito, John C. Graser, and Obaid Younossi examine the effects of changes in the test and evaluation (T&E) process used to evaluate military aircraft and air-launched guided weapons during their development programs. They also provide relationships for developing estimates of T&E costs for future programs.

- In *Software Cost Estimation and Sizing Methods: Issues and Guidelines*, MG-269-AF, 2005, Shari Lawrence Pfleeger, Felicia Wu, and Rosalind Lewis recommend an approach to improve the utility of the software cost estimates by exposing uncertainty and reducing risks associated with the developing the estimates.

- In *Lessons Learned from the F/A-22 and F/A-18 E/F Development Programs*, MG-276-AF, 2005, Obaid Younossi, David E. Stem,

Mark A. Lorell, and Frances M. Lussier evaluate historical cost, schedule, and technical information from the development of the F/A-22 and F/A-18 E/F programs to derive lessons for the Air Force and other services to improve the acquisition of future systems.

RAND Project AIR FORCE

RAND Project AIR FORCE (PAF), a division of the RAND Corporation, is the U.S. Air Force's federally funded research and development center for studies and analyses. PAF provides the Air Force with independent analyses of policy alternatives affecting the development, employment, combat readiness, and support of current and future aerospace forces. Research is conducted in four programs: Aerospace Force Development; Manpower, Personnel, and Training; Resource Management; and Strategy and Doctrine.

Additional information about PAF is available on our Web site at http://www.rand.org/paf.

Contents

Figures

Tables

Boxes

Summary

Background

The Department of Defense (DoD) forecasts its expenditures several years into the future. An important element of that forecast is the estimated cost of weapon systems, which typically take many years to acquire and remain in operation for a long time. To make those estimates, the Office of the Secretary of Defense (OSD) and the military departments use cost analysis, a discipline that attempts to forecast the ultimate cost of a weapon system far in advance of actual expenditures. But estimates are just that—estimates—not certain predictions of future costs. An analyst does not have perfect knowledge about technology, economic conditions, and other future events. Thus, a cost estimate carries with it an uncertainty and, thereby, a risk that actual costs might be higher or lower than originally anticipated.[1]

Uncertainty occurs for a number of reasons. For example, critical technical information or parameters might be unknown, poorly understood, poorly defined, or undefined when an estimate is prepared. This situation is particularly true early in a program's acquisition cycle. For example, parametric estimating methodologies for aircraft cost use characteristic factors (weight, lines of code, etc.) to forecast cost. These values might be hard to define accurately or might evolve due to changing requirements over the program's life.

---

[1] In this report, we define uncertainty as the indefiniteness in outcome—good or bad—whereas risk refers to the possibility of loss or injury, someone or something that creates or suggests a hazard, or the probability or likelihood of an adverse effect or event occurring.

Thus, the estimator must make some judgments about which values to use as a basis for estimate. Even if the actual values of these parameters could be known ahead of time, the parametric estimating method still cannot forecast cost with 100 percent certainty. Parametric forecasts contain error because parametric relationships only approximate actual cost behavior.

Uncertainty can also occur when a program uses new technologies or approaches. This situation is difficult for estimators because they have no historical analogy from which to make an estimate. Thus, an estimator must develop a new estimating approach based on limited experience or extrapolate using existing methods. New technologies and approaches also have the potential for failure, or they can encounter development difficulties leading to additional work or alternative solutions. Unfortunately, it is difficult to identify which technologies will have such problems and the resultant cost effect.

Another class of uncertainty relates to economic conditions. Some pertain specifically to a supplier or producer. For example, worker wage rates generally increase over the course of a program. However, it is difficult to forecast the magnitude of these increases because they are tied to national and local economic conditions, labor relations, and overall inflation. Another producer issue related to cost uncertainty corresponds to indirect costs. These costs, such as overhead, depend heavily on the business base of the firm. Thus, how successful the firm is in winning and holding other work not necessarily related to a program will influence indirect rates of that program.

Yet another class of uncertainty involves unusual or rare events. Examples of these types of risks are fire, earthquakes, and labor actions. Although uncommon, these types of events do occur and can have significant cost consequences on a program.

Why Is It Important to Consider Cost Uncertainty?

By and large, OSD and the military departments have historically underestimated and underfunded the cost of buying new weapon systems. Figure S.1 shows the cost growth factor (CGF) for programs dealing with systems that were similar in complexity to those procured by the Air Force (e.g., aircraft, missiles, electronics upgrades) and were either finished or nearly finished—that is, greater than 90 percent of production was completed.[2] The CGF metric is the ratio of the final cost to the estimated costs using Milestone II estimates. A CGF of less than 1.0 indicates that the initial program budget was higher than the final cost—an underrun. When the CGF exceeds 1.0, the final costs were higher than the initial budget—an overrun.

Figure S.1
Distribution of Total Cost Growth from Milestone II, Adjusted for Production Quantity Changes

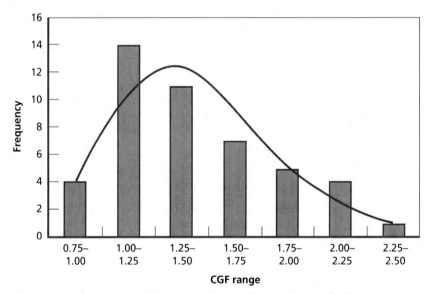

NOTE: Includes research and development, as well as production funding.
RAND MG415-S.1

---

[2] The data are drawn from Selected Acquisition Reports. They have been modified to account for inflation and changes in the number of systems produced.

xx Impossible Certainty: Cost Risk Analysis for Air Force Systems

Figure S.1 indicates both a systematic bias toward underestimating the costs and a substantial uncertainty in estimating the final cost of a weapon system. Our further analysis of the cost growth data indicates that the average adjusted total cost growth for a completed program was 46 percent from Milestone II and 16 percent from Milestone III. The bias toward cost growth does not disappear until about three-quarters of the way through production. Chapter Two of this report explores the cost growth in more detail.

Focus of This Project

In light of such cost growth and variability, senior leaders in the Air Force want to generate better cost estimates—that is, ones that provide decisionmakers with a better sense of the risk involved in the cost estimates they receive. To that end, the Air Force Cost Analysis Agency and the Air Force cost analysis community want to formulate and implement a cost uncertainty analysis policy. They asked RAND Project AIR FORCE to help. Since formulating a practical cost risk analysis policy involves more than selecting a methodology, RAND considered many issues relevant to its formulation. RAND conducted research that explored and reviewed various risk assessment methodologies that could be applied to cost estimating for major acquisition programs. RAND explored how these risk methods and policies relate to a total portfolio of programs. The research also explored how risk information can be communicated clearly to senior decisionmakers. This research was done through literature reviews; discussions with policymakers, cost estimators, and other researchers; and original research and analysis of historical cost data.

Policy Considerations

Cost uncertainty analysis is an important aspect of cost estimating and benefits decisionmaking. It helps decisionmakers understand not only the potential funding exposure but also the nature of risks for a particular program. The process can also aid in the development of more-realistic cost estimates by critically evaluating program assumptions and identifying technical issues. While we do not measure or quantify the benefits in terms of effectiveness in improving decisions and cost estimating, it is axiomatic that additional information (when correctly gathered and presented well) is of value to the decisionmaker.

A poorly done uncertainty analysis has the potential to misinform, however. Therefore, any cost uncertainty analyses should be comprehensive and based on sound analysis and data. It should consider a broad range of potential risks to a program, not just those that are currently the main concerns of the program office or contractor. Furthermore, the analysis should be rigorous and follow accepted practice for the particular method or methods employed. To the extent possible, independent technical evaluation should aid in the assessment of program cost assumptions.

The Air Force should consider several issues in formulating a cost uncertainty analysis policy:

- **A single uncertainty analysis method should not be stipulated for all circumstances and programs.** It is not practical to stipulate one specific cost uncertainty analysis methodology in all cases. Rather, the policy should offer the flexibility to use different assessment methods. Moreover, a combination of methods might be desirable and more effective in communicating risks to decisionmakers. (See pp. 35–70.)
- **A uniform communications format should be used.** A consistent display of information to senior decisionmakers can be helpful in explaining results and also allows for comparisons among programs. RAND suggests a basic three-point format (low, base, and high values) as a minimum basis for displaying risk analysis. The three points are used to show the decisionmaker a reasonable range of possible outcomes. The advantage of such an approach is that it allows for a consistent format across a variety of risk analysis methods. (See pp. 81–86.)

- **A record of cost estimate accuracy should be tracked and updated periodically.** To ensure that both the cost estimating and uncertainty analysis processes provide accurate information, estimates and assessment records should be kept and compared with final costs when those data become available. Such a process will enable organizations to identify areas where they may have difficulty estimating and sources of risk that were not adequately examined. A retrospective analysis of a program at completion would be one way to formalize the process, and the results could recommend improvements to the risk analysis process. In addition, a comparison with a previous estimate for the same system would be useful in documenting why cost estimates have changed since a previous milestone or other major decision point. It should be part of a continuous improvement effort for cost estimating. (See pp. 71–80.)
- **Risk reserves should be an accepted acquisition and funding practice.** Any policy needs to provide for a risk reserve.[3] Reserves should be used to fund costs that arise from unforeseen circumstances. However, under the current DoD and congressional acquisition and budgeting process, this recommendation will be difficult to implement. Establishing an identified risk reserve involves cultural changes in the approach to risk, not regulatory or legislative changes. Today, the only viable approach to including a reserve is burying it in the elements of the estimate. Although pragmatic, this approach has drawbacks. The burying approach will make it difficult to do retrospective analysis of whether the appropriate level of reserve was set (or the uncertainty analysis was accurate). This approach also will make it difficult to move reserves, when needed, between elements of a large program. (See pp. 71–80, 135–145.)

---

[3] Nowhere in this report do we address an approach to setting a risk reserve. For example, some have argued for a uniform 80 percent confidence level, while others have developed analytic methods (Anderson, 2003). Ultimately, we feel that the reserve needs to be set by the decisionmaker responsible for setting funding levels informed by the uncertainty assessment. The nature of the program will determine the level of the reserve, and that level will vary across programs.

Acknowledgments

First, we would like to thank Lt Gen John Corley, SAF/AQ, and Blaise Durante, SAF/AQX, for sponsoring this project. Also, we thank Richard Hartley (director) and Jay Jordan (technical director) of the Air Force Cost Analysis Agency for their help, vision, and guidance as the study unfolded.

Many people throughout the cost estimating and acquisition community deserve our gratitude for the generous sharing of their time, insight, and knowledge of the cost-risk analysis process. They are too numerous to thank individually, but we would like to at least recognize their organizations. The governmental organizations we met with were as follows:

- Air Force Aeronautical Systems Center, Cost Group
- Air Force Cost Analysis Agency
- Air Force Space and Missile Command, Cost Group
- Assistant Secretary of the Army for Cost and Economic Analysis
- Intelligence Community Cost Analysis Improvement Group
- National Aeronautics and Space Administration (NASA) Headquarters Cost Analysis Division
- NASA Jet Propulsion Laboratory
- National Reconnaissance Organization
- Naval Air Systems Command, Cost Department, AIR-4.2
- Naval Cost Analysis Division
- Missile Defense Agency

- Office of the Secretary of Defense, Program Analysis and Evaluation, Cost Analysis Improvement Group.

The nongovernmental organizations we met with were as follows:
- Aerospace Corporation
- CNA Corporation
- Harvard Center for Risk Analysis
- Institute for Defense Analyses
- Lockheed Martin Corporation
- Northrop Grumman Corporation—TASC
- MCR Federal
- MITRE Corporation
- Tecolote Research.

We are greatly indebted to the reviewers of this document—Stephen Book of MCR, Paul Garvey of MITRE, and Edward Keating and Shari Lawrence Pfleeger of RAND—whose suggestions vastly improved the quality and readability of this report. Finally, we would like to thank our RAND colleagues C. Robert Roll, Director of the RAND Project Air Force Resource Management Program, for his intellectual guidance; Robert Leonard for his help with the Selected Acquisition Report data analysis; Phillip Wirtz for editing the document; and Nathan Tranquilli for his research and administrative assistance.

Abbreviations

CAIG	Cost Analysis Improvement Group
CARD	Cost Analysis Requirements Document
CDF	cumulative distribution function
CER	cost estimating relationship
CGF	cost growth factor
CIC	cost improvement curve
DoD	Department of Defense
DoDCAS	DoD Cost Analysis Symposium
EMD	Engineering and Manufacturing Development
FSD	full-scale development
FY	fiscal year
ICE	Independent Cost Estimate
LRIP	low rate initial production
MDAP	Major Defense Acquisition Program
O&M	operations and maintenance
OSD	Office of the Secretary of Defense
PDF	probability density function
PDRR	Program Definition and Risk Reduction
PERT	Program Evaluation Review Technique
PPBS	Planning, Programming, and Budgeting System
RDT&E	research, development, test, and evaluation

SAF/AQ	Assistant Secretary of the Air Force, Acquisition
SAF/AQX	Assistant Secretary of the Air Force, Acquisition Integration
SAR	Selected Acquisition Report
SBM	scenario-based method
SCEA	Society of Cost Estimation and Analysis
TRACE	Total Risk Assessing Cost Estimate
WBS	Work Breakdown Structure

CHAPTER ONE

Introduction

This chapter begins by providing an overview of general risk analysis. Then it discusses the issue of uncertainty and risk in estimating the cost of acquisition programs. Next, it provides a brief history of cost risk analysis and an overview of what has hindered the use of cost risk estimation in the past. The chapter concludes by describing the purpose of this study, the methodology used to carry it out, and the organization of the remainder of the report.

Overview of General Risk Analysis

The terms "risk" and "uncertainty" are often confused, so it is helpful to clarify their differences. "Risk" refers to the probability of loss or injury, someone or something that creates or suggests a hazard, or the probability of an adverse effect or event. "Uncertainty" refers to the state of being unsure about something or the degree of variability in observations. In mathematical terms, it can be a statistically defined discrepancy between a measured quantity and the true value of that quantity that cannot be corrected by calculation or calibration (Bevington and Robinson, 1969). It is a measure of the caution with which the data should be used, or a measure of how poorly we understand or can predict something such as a parameter or a future behavior. Uncertainty is sometimes expressed as a probability distribution of outcomes: The greater the width of the distribution, the more uncertain the outcome. Uncertainty does not necessarily carry the same negative connotations as risk, since uncertainty may refer to a positive event.

Risk and uncertainty pervade the world. In everyday life, we encounter risks associated with, for example, investing, insurance, games or sports, gambling, weather forecasting, or simple activities such as eating, drinking, and transportation, all of which could lead to a variety of harms.

In terms of cost estimation, the field in which we are applying risk analysis, risk and uncertainty occur in several key areas. There are risks and uncertainties in estimating system requirements, understanding the maturity of technology involved, the stability of the business environment, and the proposed development and production schedules, all of which ultimately affect cost.

Risk analysis is an important component of a decisionmaking process. It allows decisionmakers to get a better understanding of the range of possible outcomes of any decision—in other words, how good or bad the outcome might be and how uncertain the outcome is. Risk analysis also helps the decisionmaking process by identifying known risk areas. In some cases, such information can be used to mitigate areas that are high risk. Risk analysis brings more information, which in turn generates more realistic expectations.

History of General Risk Analysis

Risk analysis as a part of policy analysis was first conceptualized in the 1970s and received nationwide recognition in 1983 through the publication of the seminal National Research Council's "Red Book": *Risk Assessment in the Federal Government: Managing the Process*. Two years earlier, the Society for Risk Analysis had been founded and has since expanded from its base in the United States to become an international organization.[1]

---

[1] The general field of risk analysis has been around a lot longer (e.g., in the insurance industry). For example, see Bernstein (1998).

The history of the development of risk analysis from a scholarly field to practical policy tool can be traced by a series of publications from the National Academies. The 1983 work mentioned above was the first National Academies publication that dealt with risk assessment and its role in government decisionmaking. *Improving Risk Communication* (National Research Council, 1989) advised policymakers on how best to communicate risks to the general public and explained why this was so important. *Science and Judgment in Risk Assessment* (National Research Council, 1994) focused specifically on how the U.S. Environmental Protection Agency could improve its risk assessment practices with regard to the 1990 Clean Air Act Amendments and described how scientific judgment plays a role in risk assessment. *Understanding Risk* (National Research Council, 1996) addressed a central dilemma of risk decisionmaking in a democracy: Scientific and technical information are essential for decisionmaking, but the people who make and live with those decisions are often not scientists. Therefore, the key task of risk characterization is to provide appropriate information to decisionmakers and to the public. Finally, *Toward Environmental Justice* (National Research Council, 1999) recommended that a credible, effective risk management process must involve affected citizens at all stages of the decisionmaking process.

Today, risk analysis has become both a subject of intellectual study and a tool. The range of its fields of application is enormous and includes medicine, the environment, food and water safety, technology, terrorism, finance, project management, and cost estimating.

The Components of Risk Analysis

Risk analysis has generally been divided into three broad areas: risk assessment, risk management, and risk communication. These areas are interconnected because they inform and influence each other.

Risk Assessment

Risk assessment, usually the first step in the risk analysis process, consists of identifying each risk at hand and attempting in some manner to bound or to quantify the level of potential harm. For example, risk assessment in most health, environmental, and even technological studies consists of four steps: (1) hazard identification, (2) analysis of effects, (3) exposure assessment, and (4) risk characterization—the description of the nature and often the magnitude of the risk, including the attendant uncertainty.

These are not necessarily the same steps to be followed in assessing financial or cost-related risks, but the principles are much the same. "Analysis of effects" may, in a costing problem, relate to the *magnitude* of potential cost increase if a particular outcome occurs, while "exposure assessment" is analogous to determining the *probability* that this cost increase must be borne.

Risk Management

Ruckelshaus (1985) defines *risk management* as the process by which an agency decides what action to take in the face of risk estimates. In reality, though, risks can be managed on many different levels, from the individual decisionmaker to the highest-level policymaker. Each decisionmaker must decide what constitutes "safety" or an acceptable level of risk (Rodricks and Taylor, 1983).

The risk assessment process informs risk management. At the same time, how risk is managed directly affects the risk assessment process by determining the level of risk with which the individual, group of people, or institution must live. For risk assessment to inform the risk management process in the best way, it requires a number of quality assurances (Rodricks and Taylor, 1983). First, risk analysts must make explicit all the assumptions underpinning their work and the uncertainties associated with them. Next, peer review ensures that significant departures from usual assumptions are justified. And, finally, decisionmakers, particularly those in government agencies, should ensure that the scientific assessment and the policy formulation activities remain separate so that a risk assessment is not tailored (intentionally or even subconsciously) to fit a predetermined regulatory position.

Risk assessment does not purport to give risk managers one clear answer to any problem. For example, a local government may choose to manage the risk of arsenic in municipal drinking water by requiring water utilities to reduce arsenic to ten parts per billion. Perhaps this management decision was based on a risk assessment showing that most individuals experience no adverse effect at that level, except for sensitive subpopulations. Meeting this management standard has a cost; at the same time, it may yield particular health benefits and yet still leave some subpopulations vulnerable to toxic effects. To ensure the safety of even those subpopulations, another risk management strategy may be to reduce the standard to five parts per billion. However, this decision could incur significant additional costs.

Thus, risk management almost always involves a trade-off between cost and risk or among different risks. Because many people can incur these costs and risks, risk management is not merely a set of techniques for arriving at policy decisions; it must also include informing the public about how those decisions are made (Ruckelshaus, 1985). Communication is crucial, since trust in the decision process—whether between parties or on a wider public scale—is one goal of risk management. Without understanding the basis for a decision, the public is less likely to trust that the decision made was correct.

Risk Communication

Risk communication is the process by which people or institutions with information about the risk at hand choose to communicate the risk to others—to the general public, to loved ones, or to employees, for example. Risk communication has benefited from a vast body of literature in behavioral economics and judgment and decisionmaking, which has shown that the manner in which risks are communicated can have important effects on how people react and respond to the risks.

Since the goal is to help others make more informed decisions, the field of risk communication focuses on finding methods that will enable others to understand the risks and the potential range of outcomes. Ideally, the communication process improves a rational decisionmaking process. The problem is that risk messages are difficult to formulate in ways that are accurate and clear (National Research Council, 1989). Moreover, people do not always make rational decisions, and the communication process can help or hinder this decision process. We further explore these issues in Chapters Five and Eight of this report.

Uncertainty and Risk in Cost Estimation

Cost estimation attempts to forecast the future expenditures required to develop, produce, and maintain some capital asset, hardware, service, or capability. Despite being a highly quantitative field, the values that cost estimating predicts are uncertain.[2] An estimate is a possible or likely outcome but not necessarily the actual outcome.[3] This uncertainty arises because estimators do not have perfect information about future events and because assumptions that underpin an estimate may not be accurate or well understood. For example, technical information, which often forms the basis of the cost estimate, is, at times, uncertain, undefined, or unknown when estimates are prepared. New system development may involve further uncertainty due to unproven or advanced technologies, and optimistic program assumptions can lead to extended development or the need to substitute alternative technologies.

Future economic conditions (that may affect the buyer or the seller) are another example of uncertainty that cost estimators face. Wages for workers, financing costs, taxes, overhead rates, and material cost may change as a result of conditions outside the control of the seller or buyer. The buyer also faces variable economic conditions

---

[2] The probability that any particular estimate is exactly correct is essentially zero. See Garvey (2000).

[3] In fact, some have suggested that cost estimates are more properly ranges or distributions rather than specific values (Sobel, 1965; Dienemann, 1966; DeMarco, 1982).

that could limit cash flow, thus potentially reducing future outlays and causing a program to be scaled back or rescheduled.

Another example of uncertainty is catastrophic events that, although they occur rarely, could affect final cost. Events such as a fire, strike, storm, or power failure could increase cost.[4]

Why should uncertainty in cost estimating pose a concern? Uncertainty of an estimate is tied to risk: The more uncertain the estimate, the greater the chance of an adverse or unexpected outcome. Uncertainty of an estimate can reflect both financial risk (a system requiring more money to complete than was forecasted) and operational risk (a vital capability becoming unaffordable as the program progresses). Thus, to characterize cost uncertainty is to characterize cost risk.

Understanding cost risk is an important component of decisionmaking. Decisionmakers seek to understand the risks they assume with any type of investment or program. Greater cost risk might require increased management oversight on their part, other management steps to reduce or mitigate the risks identified, or reserve funds. In the financial world, risk is usually tied to reward or return. For assuming greater risk, investors require greater potential returns. A characterization of risk is, therefore, necessary to make appropriate and rational financial decisions.

History of Cost Risk Analysis[5]

The observation that original cost estimates for projects are often not close to final costs is not, of course, new. However, after the end of World War II, the continuing military competition with the Soviet

---

[4] Note that the buyer and the seller could insure themselves against some of these events, thereby reducing financial uncertainty in the result of such an event.

[5] This brief history of cost risk analysis is based on a literature survey of more than 65 papers and books, many briefings (ranging from evaluations of the cost risk analysis field to tutorial materials presented at professional meetings), and interviews with cost analysis people in government and industry conducted for this project. Key sources are referenced in the bibliography.

Union and the need to develop successive new weapon systems led to closer attention to comparing final costs with estimates to improve management of the U.S. defense establishment. This closer scrutiny coincided with the advent of military systems analysis, growing out of the various military operations research groups from World War II and conducted at various research institutions (Garvey, 2000). This line of intellectual activity emphasized cross-disciplinary approaches to all areas of military activity, using empirical data analysis, statistics, probability modeling, and a wide variety of other mathematical tools.

The modern use of analytic techniques to examine cost risk began in the mid-1950s, with a series of studies examining the alarming propensity of weapon system projects to overrun their budgets. Much of the work in the 1950s was descriptive: tabulation of overruns or growth factors by type of platform. In their 1959 paper, Marshall and Meckling summarized a series of published and unpublished RAND work that looked at causes of cost estimation inaccuracies, such as changes in requirements, the unpredictability of developing new technology, and the lack of transparency in the formulation of estimates that would allow sources of uncertainty to be clearly understood. They also included a table of cost overrun factors for different aircraft and missile programs, with various adjustments for inflation and quantity. Marshall and Meckling (1959, p. 10) noted in a footnote that

> The data ... is particularly messy. Therefore a good deal of judgment has had to go into ... these estimates. But even after the most prudent treatment, the data ... leaves much to be desired and a good deal of caution is needed in interpreting the results.

Those familiar with cost risk analysis recognize that this comment—from the very origins of the field—could be written today.[6]

---

[6] The 1950s saw parallel intellectual developments in the field of project risk analysis, which attempted to apply rational management techniques to all aspects of project management, to include planning and tracking schedule, cost, and performance. The major innovation in the 1950s was the development of PERT (Program Evaluation Review Technique) and its appli-

In the 1960s, the growth of computing capabilities and the advancement of statistical techniques led to more-sophisticated formulations of cost risk analysis. In a series of papers, Fisher (1961, 1962) addressed the problem of explicitly dealing with uncertainty in military acquisition. He laid out a taxonomy of uncertainty and argued that, because of the lack of relevant data, in many cases "conventional" statistical methods could not be used. These papers also reviewed a number of other RAND reports that attempted to grapple with quantifying uncertainty, including a regression approach advocated by Robert Summers in 1960, called, somewhat bizarrely, the "magic formula approach." In a final evaluation, Fisher rejected most other methods in favor of sensitivity analysis to understand the effect of cost drivers, although he did note that this did not actually quantify uncertainty. However, he concluded that although some suggested methods for doing so were promising, they could not be implemented with current computing technology.

Fisher's papers were followed by researchers who advocated an explicit probability approach to cost risk assessment. Steven Sobel of MITRE and Paul Dienemann of RAND published reports (Sobel, 1965; Dienemann, 1966) that advocated treating the final cost of a project as a random variable. In this treatment, the final cost of a project, considered before the project was completed, had a probability distribution,[7] and, by estimating that distribution, many of the fundamental questions asked by managers could be answered quantitatively—for example, What was the probability that budgeting the project at a given figure would result in an eventual overrun?

---

cation to the development of the Polaris ballistic missile submarine by the U.S. Navy. Although both are closely related to cost estimation, the two fields have tended to remain professionally separate. For a history of project management, see Morris (1994).

[7] In probability theory, a real random variable such as the future cost of a system is characterized by its probability density function (PDF), which, when integrated between two points, gives the probability that the variable will lie between those two points when it is actually observed. Alternatively, the cumulative distribution function (CDF) is the integrated PDF from its lowest possible value to some value of interest. This gives the probability that the variable, when observed, will be at or below that value. For a more comprehensive explanation, see any elementary book on probability theory; for an explanation with emphasis on the application to cost analysis, see Garvey (2000).

Figure 1.1 plots the cumulative distribution function (CDF) of the final estimated cost of an illustrative project. The lowest possible value of the cost is $0, and moving to the right on the x-axis increases the probability of being below each point. In this case, there is an 80 percent probability that the final cost will be less than or equal to $280 million; correspondingly, there is a 20 percent chance that the cost will be more than $280 million. Additionally, there is a very low probability that the cost will be less than $200 million or more than $400 million.

Sobel, and especially Dienemann, extended this formulation to point out that this method indicated the risk of a project, a characteristic that is different from the expected value of the cost (in technical terms, the mean of the distribution). Dienemann gave several diagrams (often reproduced in later papers and tutorial briefings) showing a sequence of choices between two alternative projects. In one case, both projects had the same expected value; however, one had an elongated right tail, indicating a higher probability of a larger

Figure 1.1
Cost Risk as a Probability Distribution

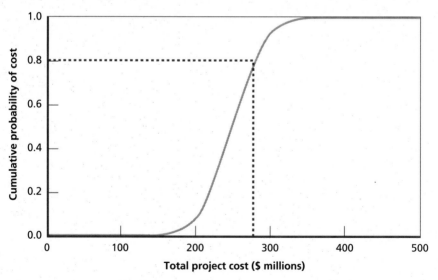

cost. The other case had one project with a higher expected cost but less risk than the alternative—that is, this second project was likely to cost less, but it had some probability of costing more. Dienemann made the general point that ultimately the decisionmaker would have to evaluate these probability distributions and decide which alternative to select, based on personal judgment.[8] This formulation of cost risk has predominated to the current time in monographs, papers, and books on cost analysis and cost risk, as well as in the associated project risk literature.[9]

The 1970s saw somewhat less innovation in techniques of cost risk, although the increasing power of computers and the more widespread availability of data led to wider application of these existing methods, in part because they were required by the government or other clients.[10] However, a sample of RAND papers on cost growth in system acquisition showed little use of the probabilistic techniques (Fisher, 1975; Perry et al., 1971; Massey, 1974).

In the 1980s, computer power continued to increase rapidly, and personal machines became widespread. In addition, predicting costs for large public and private projects received more attention, especially because of highly publicized cost overruns on many high-visibility public projects such as the English Channel Tunnel and the United States' Supersonic Transport (Morris, 1994). Probabilistic techniques were applied in some of these projects or in some parts of

---

[8] This raises a somewhat technical issue in decisionmaking, one that is largely ignored in the cost risk analysis community. Classic decision analysis requires that the outcome, whether positive or negative, be rated by *utility*, which is a measure of value to the decisionmaker (see Berger, 1980, or DeGroot, 1970, for an introduction). However, utility is not identical to dollars saved or lost, not least because there is less positive utility in underrunning by a substantial amount than negative utility in overrunning. However, this is usually ignored in the cost risk literature and straight monetary amounts are used.

[9] See Garvey (2000) and Book (2001, 2002). The field of project risk is closely related to cost risk; the primary difference being project risk focuses more broadly on quantifying both cost and schedule risk for explicit use in project management. See, for example, Cooper and Chapman (1987); Bedford and Cooke (2001), Chapter 15; Vose (2000), Chapter 13; and Williams (2002).

[10] Klementowski (1978). See also the comments on the actual use of PERT by the Polaris program in Morris (1994), p. 31, and Sapolsky (1972).

them, but again there was little critical analysis of the methodologies used and their performance. During this period, general probabilistic risk analysis became more prominent because of its connection with environmental risks, such as those posed by nuclear reactors and industrial wastes.[11]

In the 1990s, cheap computing power became ubiquitous in the United States, exceeding the requirements for most if not all cost risk methodologies and making the use of Monte Carlo simulation feasible for very large projects. This period also saw the widespread adoption of software packages (both stand-alone and add-ons to spreadsheet or project management products) that could carry out such simulations with little or no programming by a user who was an expert in substantive fields such as cost analysis.

The current state of the field has been reviewed in several books, journal articles, and presentations at professional cost analysis meetings held by the Department of Defense (DoD) and affiliated groups (the DoD Cost Analysis Symposium, or DoDCAS), the Society of Cost Estimation and Analysis (SCEA), and the International Society for Parametric Analysts.[12] In addition, much material has been collected by the Defense Acquisition University in its AT&L Knowledge Sharing System CD and Web site.[13] However, much of this literature is normative—that is, it sets out *how* cost risk analysis should be done. This is particularly true of the many briefings and tutorials given at professional cost analysis meetings, such as SCEA, Space Cost Analysis Group, and DoDCAS.[14] Little in the literature over the course of the history of cost risk analysis critically evaluates cost risk methodology in terms of effectiveness and accuracy (Galway, 2004).

---

[11] For example, see Solomon, Nelson, and Kastenberg (1983). The environmental literature is much more extensive, but scattered.

[12] Garvey (2000); Book (2001); Raymond (1999); Roberts, Smith, and Frost (2003); Shepherd (2003). The *Acquisition Review Quarterly* had a special issue in spring 2003 on these topics.

[13] Defense Acquisition University (2003a) and later versions. See http://akss.dau.mil/jsp.

[14] For example, Jarvis (2002) or Book (2002).

Obstacles to Use of Cost Risk Analysis

Despite the relatively long history of cost risk analysis and the continued portrayal of good cost risk analysis as critical to project management,[15] it is striking that the *practice* of cost risk analysis in DoD cost estimation has been spotty at best. Before proceeding to a comprehensive examination of the major cost risk assessment methods, it is worth considering the work that has documented the lack of cost risk analysis and some of the reasons that have been given for its omission.

First, it has been noted that in spite of regulations and recommendations, the use of cost risk analysis in the defense acquisition community varies widely.[16] This variation consists of projects that do and do not do cost risk analysis, as well as the use of widely varying methodologies for cost risk assessment, different practices of risk management, and inconsistent information provided in cost risk communication.

This problem is compounded by lack of specific DoD guidance on how to do a cost risk analysis.[17] While the literature and the practicing community discuss a number of methodologies, absent is any guidance on which ones are appropriate to use at different stages of a project and how well each works in different circumstances. Also, several technical issues are being debated in the community. These debates include if and how to account for dependencies among different parts of a project (i.e., correlations between the Work Breakdown Structure [WBS] elements) (Book, 2001), the form of cost

---

[15] For example, Defense Acquisition University (2003b) and online updates; the DoD 5000 series publications, which governed acquisition in the late 1990s; and briefings such as Coleman, Summerville, and Gupta (2002).

[16] Some examples of references that exhibit a wide range of dates and perspectives are Klementowski (1978); Wallenius (1985); Zsak (1997); and Conrow (2000). The variability in quality was also an almost universal opinion among our interviewees. See Driessnack, Dickover, and Smith (2003).

[17] For example, Zsak (1997). The 5000 series of DoD Instructions, which were designed to govern the DoD acquisition system, had several references to risk management and its desirability, but no information on how it should be done. Defense Acquisition University (2003b) attempts to deal with this.

estimating relationships (CERs) and their errors (Book and Young, 1997), and questions of data relevance and data adjustment, particularly for data such as those in the Selected Acquisition Reports (SARs)[18] and contractor cost data reports. All of this leads to a reluctance on the part of acquisition program managers and analysts to pursue any kind of risk analysis for their cost estimates; in the absence of guidance, almost any choice can be criticized on technical grounds by someone who does not like the answer.

The question of data availability and relevance merits more discussion. As we will discuss below, most methods of assessing cost risk require some historical data, at levels of aggregation that vary widely across the different methods. Although the SARs' data contain a substantial amount of cost data over more than a decade, there have been numerous critiques of the data, especially the SARs' high level of aggregation and the difficulty of accounting for cost changes that stem from different causes (Pannell, 1994; Jarvaise, Drezner, and Norton, 1996). The lack of standardized reporting of historical cost data is a notable obstacle to the use of cost risk analysis, because data selection can be criticized.

Some analysts contend that senior decisionmakers do not understand risk analysis as applied to cost risk. Although this opinion was in the minority among our interviewees, there is a strong perception that decisionmakers largely do not trust cost risk analysis because current methodologies do not provide them with the information they need for their decisions. As noted above, risk communication was the last element of risk analysis to be recognized as vital by the general risk analysis community, and it has proved to be arguably the most

---

[18] The SARs are periodic summaries (normally annual) of program technical characteristics, contract information, actual and projected quantities, actual costs incurred to date, estimated future costs, projected costs by year, and so forth. They are developed by the program office, approved by OSD, and submitted to Congress as part of the President's Budget submission each year. Other SARs must be completed quarterly if a program cost or schedule growth exceeds certain criteria. See 10 U.S.C. Section 2432 for details.

difficult part of the job.[19] This aspect of cost risk analysis has received comparatively little attention and was a separate task in this project.

The acceptance of cost risk analysis is also hampered by the lack of publicly available, empirical work documenting its effectiveness in making management decisions.[20] As Hillson (1998) and Galway (2004) both noted, in the closely related area of project management there is a fairly large pedagogical literature on how to do risk analysis (tutorials, texts, field overviews with toy examples, etc.) and a somewhat smaller set of works that decry its neglect by decisionmakers. However, according to both authors, virtually no works offer specifics on applying risk techniques to real projects and real cost risks, and none evaluate the performance of these methods in helping decisionmakers and managers make more accurate decisions.

The final and in some ways most formidable obstacle to cost risk analysis is political. In some cases, project leaders or senior decisionmakers do not want a rigorous objective cost risk analysis because of the possibility that it will cause a favored project to be canceled.

Purpose of This Study

As stated previously, over many years the field of cost estimating has developed methods to quantify estimate risk and uncertainty. Typically, these methods are statistically based (e.g., Monte Carlo). That is, these methods determine a cost probability distribution for a cost estimate. But the question arises as to what is the appropriate cost risk methodology to use. Should different methods be used for different circumstances (e.g., during different program phases)? Do these methods adequately address overall cost risk and provide the desired information? How should this cost risk information be communi-

---

[19] Slovic (1986); Plough and Krimsky (1987); National Research Council (1989); Morgan et al. (2002).

[20] However, there have been extensive studies on the value of risk analysis and management outside of the cost field. See, for example, Mayo and Hollander (1991).

cated to senior decisionmakers? Our research addresses these questions.

The purpose of this research is to aid the Air Force Cost Analysis Agency and the Air Force cost analysis community in formulating and implementing a cost risk policy. RAND explored and reviewed various risk methodologies that could be applied to cost estimating for major acquisition programs. Furthermore, RAND looked into how these cost risk methods and policies relate to a total portfolio of programs. The research also explored how cost risk estimates can be communicated to senior decisionmakers in a clear and understandable way. However, we did not study the implications of cost risk analysis to funding and budgeting decisions.

This research was done through literature reviews; discussions with policymakers, costs estimators, and other researchers; and original research and analysis of historical cost data.

How We Went About Conducting This Study

To answer the above questions, we divided the research into the following six tasks.

Task 1: An Analysis of Weapon System Cost Growth

To set the context regarding the magnitude of cost growth as well as using cost growth as a proxy for cost risk, we explored the historical experience of cost growth on acquisition programs. Over the years, RAND has developed a database built on the SARs. Using these data with some supplementary information, we examined cost growth history to understand whether there are factors that correlate with cost growth. Furthermore, other studies have been done on program cost growth, and we reviewed this literature and compared their findings.

Task 2: A Review of Risk/Uncertainty Assessment Methodologies

Several fields other than cost estimating employ methods for quantifying risk. These areas are diverse and include financial investing, medical research and treatment, and capital expenditure. We reviewed these approaches and evaluated their applicability to cost esti-mating on military acquisitions. We also explored and reviewed vari-ous approaches to quantifying cost risk on acquisition programs.

Task 3: The Cognitive Psychology of Risk Assessment

The field of cognitive psychology has examined how humans perceive and judge risk. For example, it is generally felt that people do not characterize the relative risks of various activities appropriately. What are the implications of this research in terms of cost analysis? One possible implication is that if people cannot objectively perceive risk, they cannot estimate its effect. For this task, we review some of the literature and discuss what it implies in terms of cost risk analysis.

Task 4: Risk Management for a Collection of Programs

To this point, the tasks have focused on a single program risk evalua-tion. However, the Air Force must manage many acquisition pro-grams. What are the implications for cost risk analysis when looking at a collection of programs? What is an appropriate cost risk policy for the Air Force when considering a collection of programs? For this task, we explored policies for a collection of programs. We reviewed work in such fields as finance (portfolio theory) for appropriate poli-cies and examined its potential applicability to Air Force acquisitions.

Task 5: Communication of Cost Risk to Decisionmakers

Traditionally, cost risk has been communicated through statistics. Often, decisionmakers are not trained or well versed in statistics, thus making their understanding of the implied cost risk difficult. This task examined alternative methods to present the results of risk analy-sis in a simple yet meaningful way. We conducted systemic structured interviews of key individuals who have received program milestone cost estimates to gain a better understanding of their needs and the issues in understanding cost risk assessments. Also, we assessed how cost risk is communicated in other fields and reviewed existing research on this topic.

Task 6: Considerations for a Cost Risk Policy
This task synthesizes the research in the five previous tasks and makes policy recommendations.

How This Report Is Organized

Following this introduction, Chapter Two traces the history of cost growth in military acquisition programs as a way of defining the scope of the cost estimation problem. Chapter Three presents a summary of general risk analysis methods. Chapter Four illustrates the diversity of risk analysis techniques applied in cost estimating. Chapter Five summarizes the issues related to cost risk analysis from a senior decisionmaker's perspective. Chapter Six discusses the problem of presenting the results of cost risk estimation to decisionmakers and recommends an approach. Chapter Seven presents our conclusions and observations, including the considerations in implementing a cost risk estimation policy. This report also contains seven appendixes. Appendix A shows the acquisition programs included in our cost growth analysis. Appendix B lists the people we interviewed for this study. Appendix C contains a set of questions for cost analysts to consider when developing a cost risk analysis. Appendix D presents some findings from cognitive psychology that shed light on how psychological biases can affect risk estimation. Appendix E discusses some of the issues involved in managing the risk for a collection of programs compared with a single program. Appendix F discusses applying the scenario-based method to a three-point communications format. Appendix G provides the milestone definitions used by the researchers.

CHAPTER TWO
History of Cost Growth

Does DoD have a problem with its cost estimates, and, if so, what is the magnitude of the problem? To answer that question, RAND Project AIR FORCE researchers analyzed data contained in the SARs database. This chapter summarizes those results, and a more extensive treatment of the SAR cost growth data can be found in a future RAND publication.

It should be noted that cost estimating uncertainty and cost growth are not necessarily the same thing. Cost growth can occur for a number of reasons, some of which are not related to the estimating process. For example, the government might choose to accelerate a program or increase production quantities to meet an urgent operational need that was not originally envisioned. Conversely, a program might be slowed because of budget constraints or other priorities. Cost growth represents the *funding* uncertainty. Cost risk and uncertainty are specific to a particular program's technical content and estimating assumptions. In terms of distributions, one might expect cost growth to have a broader distribution than cost estimating uncertainty.

Cost Growth Data

SARs are annual reports that summarize the current program status for major defense programs (Drezner et al., 1993). These reports provide an aggregated means of monitoring cost and schedule performance of all Major Defense Acquisition Programs (MDAPs) of DoD.[1] The SAR data constitute one of the better ways to track cost estimates and schedules for major defense programs. Over the past several years, RAND has collected and organized cost data from these reports as a basis for understanding and characterizing cost growth. Currently, the data collected by RAND are organized into a database comprising more than 150 programs with SAR information from 1968 through 2003. The database focuses mainly on cost, schedule, quantity, and categorical[2] data from the SARs.[3]

Using SAR data to study cost growth has several limitations. Although these reasons have been thoroughly discussed elsewhere, it is worthwhile to summarize some of these limitations (Hough, 1992).

- **Data are reported at high levels of aggregation.** The cost data contained in the SARs are at a high level of aggregation (e.g., development, production, military construction) so that doing in-depth cost growth analysis (e.g., at a WBS level) is not possible.
- **Baseline changes, modifications, and restructuring are not well documented.** The original, baseline program on which the cost estimate is based evolves or changes as the program matures and uncertainties are resolved. However, this shifting baseline hampers the study of cost growth across programs. Not all programs make similar or consistent baseline shifts, and the choice of the "correct" baseline from which to measure growth is often ambiguous.
- **Reporting guidelines and requirements change.** Over the years that SARs have been prepared, the thresholds and report-

---

[1] MDAPs are DoD acquisition programs estimated by the Office of the Under Secretary of Defense for Acquisition, Technology, and Logistics to require an eventual total expenditure for research, development, test, and evaluation of more than $365 million in fiscal year (FY) 2000 constant dollars or, for procurement, of more than $2.190 billion in FY 2000 constant dollars. See DoD Instruction 5000.2 for more information.

[2] These data include lead service, contractor, system type, and aspects of the development strategy.

[3] For more information on the database, see Jarvaise, Drezner, and Norton (1996).

ing guidelines have evolved. Thus, comparing data across time periods can be challenging. This problem is particularly important when looking for trends.

- **Allocations of cost growth variances are inconsistent.** The SARs allocate the difference between the baseline estimate and current estimate into one of seven variance categories: economic, quantity, estimating, engineering, schedule, support, and other. Although there are guidelines on how to allocate cost growth to these categories, the allocation is sometimes not consistent among programs and therefore not helpful in determining the causes for the variance.

- **Weapon system costs are incomplete.** Sometimes, the SAR data for a program may not comprise the total system cost. For example, the earlier ship programs separated system and shipbuilding costs. Thus, the cost growth for such a programs may be misstated by looking only at one component of the total cost.

- **Certain types of programs are excluded.** Not all DoD programs prepare SARs. Those below the reporting threshold (by cost) do not have them. Furthermore, highly classified, special access programs are not included in the reports. Some programs received exemptions for other reasons.

- **The basis of the cost estimate is often ambiguous.** While the reported estimate in the SAR is the official program office position, the basis is somewhat unclear. The estimate reported in the annual SAR must match the funding contained in the President's Budget for that reporting period but may not represent the most recent cost estimate. Using the SAR data to analyze estimating performance through cost growth is somewhat tenuous. The values may represent the estimate by the program office, contract, independent group, service, or Office of the Secretary of Defense (OSD) budget organizations—or some combination.

- **Risk reserves are unidentified.** Some programs include risk reserve funds to offset potential cost growth. These funds are meant to cover expected cost increases that may happen for a variety of reasons. Because unallocated funds or allowances are targets for budget cuts, risk reserve (if included) is usually "buried" somewhere in the estimate and not separately identified. One program might experience low cost growth relative to another because it has a greater reserve in its baseline estimate, despite having similar technical and programmatic risk.

Analytic Approach

Notwithstanding these shortfalls, the SARs represent the most consistent collection of program and cost data available on DoD acquisition programs and do accurately report the growth in program costs over time. The SAR data have been an invaluable tool for cost research and have been used for several studies done by RAND and others in the cost analysis field.[4] Many of these studies focused on some aspects of weapon system cost growth, such as characterizing growth, examining trends, and looking for correlations with cost growth. As stated before, the focus of this study is to characterize cost estimate uncertainty; therefore, we concentrate on quantifying and characterizing cost growth more than explaining it.

Sample Selection

For this analysis, we have used a subset of information in the full RAND SAR database. We used two criteria to select programs for the sample. First, we chose a subset of programs that dealt with systems of complexity similar to those procured by the Air Force (e.g., aircraft, missiles, electronics upgrades) and excluded those that did not (e.g., ships). From these programs, we selected programs that have finished (or that were nearly finished—i.e., greater than 90 percent production complete). Thus, we excluded ongoing programs or ones that had been canceled. This second criterion was used to make cer-

---

[4] For example, see Drezner et al. (1993); McNicol (2004); and Tyson, Harmon, and Utech (1994).

tain we could determine the "true" or "actual" final costs and not some projection.[5] Appendix A lists the programs selected.

Cost Growth Metric

As our metric for cost growth, we chose the cost growth factor (CGF). This metric is the ratio of the final cost to the originally estimated costs; thus, each estimate or baseline has a different CGF (the numerator is constant, but the denominator changes). Therefore, it is important to state the estimate baseline to place the CGF in context. For the most part, we present CGFs relative to a specific milestone for the program (described more fully in the next section). A CGF of 1 indicates that the estimate equaled the final cost; a CGF less than 1 indicates that the estimate was higher than the final cost—an underrun; and a CGF greater than 1 indicates that the final costs were higher than the estimate—an overrun.

Note that the CGF is a ratio that does not cover all values. Values less than zero are not possible. To have a negative CGF would imply that the government was paid to acquire a system—clearly an unrealistic situation. Given the truncation at zero, one might expect that the statistical distributions of CGF would not be normal. Later, we will explore the form of the CGF distribution as part of this research.

Normalization

When calculating a metric based on a broad population of data, it is necessary to adjust the data so that individual observations are comparable. We have made two important adjustments to the data, one for inflation and the other for the final quantities produced. To cal-

---

[5] Not including canceled programs does mean that we have likely underestimated the actual cost growth for programs. This underestimation results from the fact that canceled programs are largely terminated for having extreme cost growth. However, without final cost data, we cannot quantify what the actual growth would have been for those programs, only the growth at the time the program was terminated.

culate CGFs, we use the base-year cost values reported in the SARs. Thus, the CGFs have changes due to inflation largely removed.[6]

The second adjustment is to modify the estimated production cost for the final number of units produced. Often, the number of units produced for a program changes after a milestone decision. Quantities could decrease because of budget constraints, other emerging funding priorities, or as a method of cost control. Similarly, an urgent or increased operational need could result in more units being produced than originally planned. Therefore, very significant swings can occur in production cost due to the actual quantity produced being much different than originally planned, which may or may not affect the estimated unit cost. Such changes in quantities are difficult to forecast.

To remove the effects of quantity changes, we adjusted all the SAR production cost estimates to the final quantity produced. The adjustment was done using the cumulative cost improvement curve (CIC) (slope and first-unit cost values) provided in each SAR as the basis for an adjusted estimate. We recalculated the production cost estimate using the final quantity produced and the CIC values from a particular estimate. The adjusted production values are similar to a point in the original estimate where the final quantities would have occurred.[7] However, we also present values for unadjusted quantity as well. The unadjusted CGFs are useful because they represent the "funding" uncertainty. The quantity-adjusted CGFs provide a better representation of the "estimate" uncertainty.[8]

---

[6] Admittedly, it is quite difficult to make perfect adjustments for inflation or create general escalation indexes that represent a number of programs' unique situations. Nonetheless, calculations using base-year values should largely remove the major effects of inflation and are done using a standard set of DoD inflation rates.

[7] We have made no correction for rate of production, which also can be affected when quantity is changed.

[8] See Drezner et al. (1993).

Cost Growth Analysis

In this section, we characterize CGF for the SAR data. Again, the purpose of this chapter is to provide information to cost analysts so that they may make simple risk assessments based on the historical data or calibrate a risk analysis done by other methods. We segment the data by funding category, milestone, and commodity type to accommodate different approaches. For most of the data, we display simple summary statistics.

Segmented CGF Results

Milestones. The current U.S. acquisition system follows a "gated" review process, where formal approvals are needed to begin certain activities. These gates are referred to as milestones. The programs analyzed for cost growth fit the older acquisition system nomenclature (Milestones I, II, and III). Milestone I is the point where programs are approved to undertake Program Definition and Risk Reduction (PDRR) activities. Milestone II is the approval to enter into the Engineering and Manufacturing Development (EMD) phase. Milestone III is the approval to enter into production, fielding/deployment, and operations and support. The milestones allow us to compare programs at approximately similar times (i.e., when the maturity should be similar).[9]

---

[9] Most of the time, our selection of the milestone baseline estimate (i.e., the particular SAR estimate that we designate as the baseline) is consistent with the actual baseline published in the SAR. However, there are cases in which we have deviated from that published baseline because we wanted to be consistent:

- Across decades where acquisition system has changed definitions and structure. Often the point that is designated by the baseline changes or shifts based on how the acquisition process is currently defined.
- Between types of acquisitions as certain weapon systems (e.g., ships) designate milestones differently from other types of programs.
- Where a program baseline is modified (i.e., the program estimate has a new baseline set).

To maintain consistency, we use a commitment-driven approach (i.e., when money is obligated) tied to major contract award points to define milestone baselines. For example, once a major contract for engineering and manufacturing development or full-scale development is

Note that the milestones we use differ from the current acquisition system. However, since we are using historical data, we use the milestone nomenclature current at the time the programs were being acquired; we make no attempt to adjust or redefine them to the current DoD acquisition system. See DoD Instruction 5000.2 for a description of the current milestone decision points.

Funding Category. The SAR cost data are broken out into the following categories:

- Development—(or, more formally, RDT&E) funds spent for research, development, test, and evaluation (for the Air Force all 3600 monies)
- Procurement—funds spent for all units (end item) of the weapon system acquired (for the Air Force 3010 monies for aircraft and 3020 monies for missiles). Development units are included in the development cost
- Military construction—construction of facilities (e.g., buildings, ground stations) related to the weapon system
- Operations and maintenance (O&M)—funds spent for operations and maintenance work in support of acquisition
- Total cost—the summation of all the above categories (i.e., development, procurement, military construction, and O&M).

Because the data for O&M costs are almost always missing or not applicable, we do not analyze the category separately; however, we include it as part of the total cost category, where appropriate. A further difficulty with the O&M costs is that SAR reporting normally ends when a system has either completed 90 percent of the total program quantities or spent 90 percent of the total program funding. At that point, the collection of O&M costs is immature because most systems have an operational life of ten years or more after production has ended. As described above, we calculate two CGFs for produc-

awarded, we designate that point to be Milestone II, irrespective of future changes or approvals. For further detail, see Appendix G.

tion: one adjusted and another unadjusted for quantity changes. As a result, we also display two CGFs for total cost—adjusted and unadjusted for quantity. Table 2.1 (p. 29) shows the summary statistics for each of the categories using the Milestone II SAR estimate as the baseline.

The statistics in Table 2.1 raise some interesting points. The first is that there is a consistent underestimation of cost (a bias toward underestimating). Both the mean and median for each of the categories are well above 1. Another point is that the distributions are skewed toward the upper side. This can be noted from the fact that the mean is consistently higher than the median. Another point to note is the decrease for the mean, standard deviation, and minimum and maximum ranges when comparing the adjusted production and total numbers with the unadjusted numbers. On average, production quantities grew by approximately 30 percent for the sample—hence the larger values for the unadjusted growth.

The shape of the CGF distribution allows us to gauge the magnitude of the variability and thus the approximate uncertainty of estimates. Figure 2.1 shows the distribution of the CGFs for adjusted total growth with Milestone II as the baseline. The bars on the chart represent the frequency distribution of the data sample. The solid line is a lognormal fit to the data using the mean and standard deviation of the sample in logspace—0.34 and 0.26, respectively. Note that the lognormal distribution is a fairly good but not perfect fit. The actual distribution seems to be a bit more peaked and has a slightly flatter tail than the fitted distribution. However, these differences from the lognormal fit could be due to the small sample size of 46 points, or it could be that the relationship is more complex than one of the standard distributions.

Table 2.2 displays the summary statistics for each of the categories using the Milestone III SAR estimate as the baseline. The general trends resemble those of Milestone II, but the CGFs are lower and have less variability than do the Milestone II values, as one might expect for a milestone occurring later in a program. As noted in the

Figure 2.1
Distribution of Total Cost Growth from Milestone II, Adjusted for Production Quantity Changes

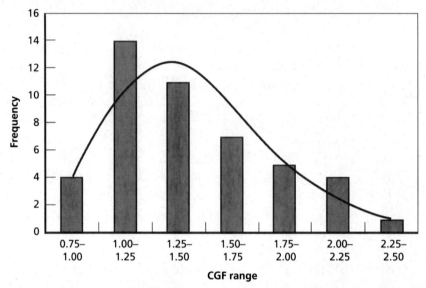

NOTE: Includes research and development, as well as production funding.
RAND *MG415-2.1*

table, one observation significantly skewed the military construction mean and standard deviation. An important observation is that development costs continue to grow after Milestone III, even though one would expect significant development efforts to be nearly complete as a program enters full rate production. This growth might be a result of requirements growth, performance upgrades, or technology update activities.

The RAND 1993 study on cost growth also reported a similar breakdown of CGFs. Table 2.3 shows a comparison of the means for CGFs for Milestone II SAR reported by this study and the 1993 study. Note that it was not possible to compare all the categories in Tables 2.1 and 2.2 because the 1993 study did not report them.

Table 2.1
CGF Summary Statistics by Funding Categories from Milestone II

Category	Number of Observations	Mean	Median	Standard Deviation	Minimum	Maximum
Total (adjusted)	46	1.46	1.44	0.38	0.77	2.30
Total (unadjusted)	46	1.65	1.25	1.08	0.37	5.56
Development	46	1.58	1.34	0.79	0.77	5.47
Procurement (adjusted)	44	1.44	1.40	0.42	0.51	2.29
Procurement (unadjusted)	44	1.73	1.30	1.37	0.28	7.28
Military construction	10	1.33	1.11	0.82	0.51	2.87

Table 2.2
CGF Summary Statistics by Funding Categories from Milestone III

Category	Number of Observations	Mean	Median	Standard Deviation	Minimum	Maximum
Total (adjusted)	68	1.16	1.13	0.26	0.48	2.30
Total (unadjusted)	68	1.25	1.04	0.79	0.31	5.01
Development	65	1.30	1.10	0.64	0.89	5.47
Procurement (adjusted)	68	1.19	1.17	0.33	0.29	2.52
Procurement (unadjusted)	69	1.27	1.01	1.06	0.01	6.36
Military construction	26	5.26[a]	0.77	22.31[a]	0.11	117.00

[a] One high growth observation (value of 117) significantly skews the mean higher. Without this observation, the mean is 0.81 and the standard deviation is 0.51.

Table 2.3
A Comparison of the CGF Means for Milestone II Between This Study and the 1993 RAND Study

Category	Current Study	1993 Study
Total (adjusted)	1.46	1.30
Development	1.58	1.25
Procurement (adjusted)	1.44	1.18
Procurement (unadjusted)	1.73	N/A

An increase of about 0.16 to 0.33 occurs for the categories between the 1993 study and this study. Nevertheless, we cannot conclude that the previous data analysis is in error. The baseline data and quantity adjustment factors were nearly the same. However, there were a few important differences. The quantity adjustment procedures for the 1993 study differed somewhat from the ones used here. The 1993 study used the cost variance data reported in the SARs to adjust for quantity changes; in this study, we used the quantity normalization procedure described earlier. Another major difference lies in the sample of programs. The early study included all programs in the database at least three years past the start of EMD (Milestone II), whereas this one selected only completed programs. Thus, the 1993 study would have had estimates for many programs in development or production, not the final costs. This difference certainly suggests that including only completed programs is necessary to reflect the final CGFs. We have excluded a few types of programs from the analysis, which could also contribute to the difference between the studies.

Milestone. One might expect that as a program passes through successive milestones, the mean of the CGFs should tend toward 1 and the standard deviation should decrease. In other words, the estimates should become more accurate as the program matures. Indeed, these trends appear in the data. Table 2.4 shows the CGF for adjusted total cost by milestone, and Table 2.5 shows the unadjusted values.

Table 2.4
CGF for Adjusted Total Growth, by Milestone

Milestone	Mean	Standard Deviation	Number of Observations
I	1.46	0.50	5
II	1.45	0.36	43
II/III	1.59	0.65	3
III	1.14	0.21	65

Table 2.5
CGF for Unadjusted Total Growth, by Milestone

Milestone	Mean	Standard Deviation	Number of Observations
I	1.86	1.20	5
II	1.60	0.98	43
II/III	2.33	2.32	3
III	1.20	0.65	65

Note that there is a combined Milestone II/III category for programs that passed through both milestones in a single year. These programs had accelerated or early production. Given the small number of observations for the Milestone I and the combined Milestone II/III, it is difficult to make a definitive statement on the progression between all the milestones. Yet a clear progression in both mean and standard deviation occurs between Milestones II and III.

Correlations

We wanted to determine which aspects of the program correlated with cost growth and therefore analyzed the data statistically to identify them. We note that correlation does not necessarily imply causality. We explored correlations by development, procurement, and total cost growth with different factors.[10] We report only correlations with a statistically significant difference. With respect to development costs at Milestone II, we observed three significant correlations: a trend with time, a difference among commodity types, and a trend with duration. Interestingly, Milestone III development CGFs do not have the same trend, but many reasons could account for this difference (e.g., most of the initial research and development costs are known by Milestone III). There are very few correlations with procurement cost growth. Electronics programs have lower cost growth, at least for the Milestone II estimates. The data also show a trend of higher procurement CGFs for programs with longer times between Milestone II and the final SAR (production at least 90 percent complete point). The correlations for total cost growth follow a similar pattern to those for development and procurement. For the growth from Milestone II, a slight downward trend occurs with the year that Milestone II occurred. For the more recent programs, however, their durations tend to be much shorter than the rest of the sample. For example, programs starting in the mid-1990s could not have a duration of more than ten years if the program is finished (a criterion for inclusion in the analysis). Therefore, it is *not* possible to conclude that total cost growth has improved with time in recent decades. We did not observe a significant trend by program size (total cost) or by service.

Observations

Our analysis of the SAR data indicates that completed programs show about a 20 percent higher growth than does the full database of completed and in-process programs. The average adjusted total cost growth for a completed program was 46 percent from the Milestone II cost estimate and 16 percent from Milestone III. It should be

---

[10] We explored factors such as service (i.e., Air Force, Army, or Navy), program size (total value), commodity type (e.g., aircraft, missile, munitions), percentage development cost, and time (milestone year).

noted that this cost growth *underestimates* potential future cost growth, since we have omitted programs that were canceled (primarily for having large cost growth). The bias toward cost growth does not disappear until about three-quarters of the way through production, at which point actual production costs should be well known. Also, programs that had longer durations experienced greater cost growth. Electronics programs tended to have lower cost growth. We found no significant differences in CGFs due to program size or service.

CHAPTER THREE

A Review of General Risk Methods

The analysis of risk is increasingly being viewed as a discipline in itself, and there is high demand for an orderly and formal treatment of risk in the general areas of public health and safety and business decisionmaking, as well as in DoD acquisition. This chapter gives a primer on various risk analysis methods and then treats in more detail the important role of risk analysis methods in the field of cost analysis.

Risk Assessment Methods

Depending on the nature of the risk and the availability of historical or real-time data, a variety of risk assessment methods can be used to attempt to bound or quantify the risk. We very briefly describe the following methods of general risk analysis below:

- Benefit-cost analysis
- Expert judgment
- Fault tree analysis
- Focus groups/one-on-one interviews
- Root cause analysis
- Behavior modeling
- Data-based methods
- Integrated assessment.

Following these descriptions, we give more-detailed treatments of variants of these methods that are most relevant to cost risk analysis.

Benefit-Cost Analysis

Benefit-cost analysis involves a set of procedures for defining and comparing the benefits with the costs of a particular risky event or undertaking; in this sense, it serves as a way of organizing and analyzing data for decisionmaking (Zerbe and Dively, 1994). The role of the benefit-cost practitioner is to analyze effects of risks and their monetary values to inform the policymaking process. These values are important because they allow decisionmakers to compare benefits of a particular strategy or course of action with the potential risks directly using the same measure—dollars (Freeman, 1979). A complete benefit-cost analysis makes explicit the assumptions about the values of benefits and costs embedded in different policy choices (Environmental Protection Agency, 2000). However, one of the drawbacks of this method is that benefits and risks may be difficult to quantify. For example, the loss of aesthetic value due to development of woodlands would be difficult to quantify.

Expert Judgment

Expert judgment is applied to future situations where risk cannot be predicted accurately based on historical data but can be bounded. (For example, expert judgment is often called upon regarding future risk of climate change.) This method is also appropriate for risks that occur with such low frequency or with such irregularity (e.g., earthquakes in Taiwan) that precise probabilities cannot be quantitatively found. There are several techniques to implementing expert judgment, such as direct solicitation of individual experts, focus groups, and the Delphi method. These methods vary in how the expert's opinion is solicited—from individual discussion, to group discussions, to formalized voting.

A weakness of the expert judgment method is that experts often disagree, and it is not clear how to weigh and combine the various expert opinions to get a single answer (Morgan, 1981). Furthermore, experts may be just as prone as laypersons to biases that distort their estimates (Ruckelshaus, 1985).

Fault Tree Analysis

Fault tree analysis is applied in situations where multiple potential risks can lead to a specific adverse outcome(s). It takes into account the dynamic (timing and dependence/correlation) aspects of the situation into account. It is relevant to situations where causes of risk vary over time. If only one type of risk leads to one outcome, then this is not the most appropriate method. Also, this method is useful only when it is possible to assign probabilities of risk with a high level of precision.

Fault trees are used most often to characterize hazards for which direct experience is not available. The method may be used to map all relevant possibilities and to determine the probability of the final outcome. To accomplish the latter goal, the probabilities of all component events or risks, as well as their logical connections, must be completely specified (Slovic, Fischhoff, and Lichtenstein, 1979).

Focus Groups/One-on-One Interviews

Focus groups, in which a moderator leads a group of people in discussion on a given risk, are applied in situations where participants may have different views. These groups are a good setting in which to learn about the range of views and to allow participants to explain the reasoning behind these views. It is also appropriate in settings where consensus is valued. One-on-one interviews are similar to the focus group approach, except that these interviews are more appropriate for individual risk behaviors rather than community-based ones (e.g., whether patients actually follow their doctors' recommended regime for antibiotics).

Root Cause Analysis/Failure Modes and Effects Analysis

Root cause analysis is a process that attempts to identify underlying causes of negative outcomes.[1] It is most appropriate for situations

---

[1] See, for example, Rooney and Vanden Heuvel (2004).

where specific risk events or errors have already occurred and data on these events are available, making it possible to do a detailed audit of the history of circumstances that led to the event. Fields such as safety, heath, environment, quality, reliability, and production apply to this process. The process involves four basic steps: (1) data collection, (2) causal factor charting, (3) root cause identification, and (4) recommendations. The unique aspects of this process are steps 2 and 3, both of which are graphical techniques. For causal factor charting, the sequence of events that led to the negative outcome (as identified during the data collection) is mapped. From this map, a set of causal factors is identified. The root cause identification step examines the underlying reasons for each of these causal factors. The advantage of the formal process is that it forces investigators to be systematic in the identification of risk sources and to evaluate all possible causes, not simply the most obvious ones.

Failure modes analysis and effects analysis employ the same techniques as root cause analysis in that they examine the consequences of failures or risk (and chains of them). However, these approaches are used prospectively to examine overall risks and to identify potential weakness; they are typically used in safety-critical systems, such as nuclear power plants and commercial aircraft.

Behavior Modeling

This method is applied in situations where there is a good understanding of the cognitive or motor processes involved in producing the behavior that can result in an adverse outcome. In regard to risk events and public participation, Aaron Wildavsky (1979) points out: "Why, if accidents or health rates are mainly dependent on personal behavior, does the vast bulk of governmental resources go into engineering safety in the environment rather than inculcating it into the individual?" Indeed, knowing more about how people think, feel, and know about a particular risk may in some cases be the most effective part of designing a risk management procedure.

Data-Based Methods

Data-based methods, such as descriptive displays or regression analyses, are appropriate when the number of errors or adverse outcomes and the circumstances under which they occur can be recorded. The goal of data-based methods is to use statistical techniques to find out the relative contribution of potential contributing factors to the observed incidence of errors or adverse outcomes. One method of descriptive analysis is the *tornado plot* (Coopersmith et al., 2000/ 2001), in which the set of relative contributions of each factor to an outcome is ranked visually by putting the factor with greatest contribution at top, followed by the next greatest contributing factor, etc.[2] Regression analysis is another technique that can be used to provide quantitative measures of correlation between adverse outcomes and possible contributing factors. For example, regression models have been developed for cost growth on process plant investments (Merrow, Philips, and Myers, 1981).

Integrated Assessment

Integrated assessment is used in situations where it is possible to use a combination of approaches to assess the likelihood of a particular adverse outcome. An example of such a situation is the threat of cryptosporidium, a protozoan parasite, in drinking water (Small et al., 2002). Expert judgment was used to quantify conditions that lead to cryptosporidium outbreaks, based on an understanding of natural phenomena (e.g., flood conditions near cattle farms) and institutional behavior (e.g., water utilities detecting contamination; public health officials getting the word out to citizens). This approach was combined with human behavior modeling, based on an understanding of how people deal with their drinking water (e.g., Do people follow boil-water advisories?) to determine the likely size of an outbreak of cryptosporidiosis.

---

[2] Since the contributions decrease as the factors go down, the plot has a characteristic funnel shape—hence the name.

Observations

A number of themes and issues arise from implementation of these general methodologies. The most important ones are related to (1) the possible precision or validity of risk estimation; (2) the level of control professional staff have over risk factors; (3) the extent to which individuals or a particular community is involved in the risk management process; (4) the extent to which risks and errors occur as independent events or as part of a dynamic sequence of events; (5) the extent to which one risk contributes to one adverse outcome, or whether a series of errors leads to this outcome; (6) the extent to which it is possible to record risks and the circumstances under which they occur; and (7) the extent to which the human performance contribution to risk is understood.

CHAPTER FOUR

Risk Analysis in Cost Estimation

Before moving to the application of risk analysis concepts to the analysis of cost risk, it is worth stepping back to consider the purpose of cost estimation in DoD acquisition and the characteristics that require the use of risk analysis to supplement the basic activity of cost estimation.

Cost estimates provide decisionmakers with needed information for a variety of choices that have to be made over the course of an acquisition. For example:

- What are the costs of different acquisition alternatives?
- What is an adequate budget for an acquisition program?
- Are contractor proposals for the program realistic?
- If a program is under way, is it costing more than the estimate, leading to a potential need for more resources, perhaps from other sources?

As stated in a previous chapter, the problem with cost estimation is that cost estimators lack perfect information about the future, and therefore forecasts can be off for many reasons. To help solve these issues, cost risk analysis applies risk analysis methods to evaluate the uncertainty of cost estimates and communicate this uncertainty to decisionmakers. On the basis of that information, the decisionmakers can decide whether a program is too risky to initiate or even continue, and whether funding is adequate to cover some or all of the likely hazards that may occur. Often, decisionmakers also want a cost risk analysis to indicate the relative probability and consequences of specific risks of particular interest, both to indicate which are covered by different budgets and to help set priorities on risk mitigation efforts. This process is much like general risk analysis, covered previously, and indeed the purpose, methodologies, and framework used are quite similar.[1]

For the purpose of this report, we use the following definitions:

- *Cost risk*: potential increased cost due to possible occurrence of an uncertain hazard, which accounts for both the consequences (size of the increase) and the probability of the consequences
- *Cost uncertainty*: the degree of indefiniteness about a particular estimate or value (i.e., the range of possible outcomes)
- *Cost risk analysis*: the process of assessing, characterizing, and communicating cost risk
- *Cost risk assessment*: the identification and quantification of a specific cost risk or uncertainty.

Review of Cost Risk Methodologies

We now turn to a detailed examination of specific cost risk assessment methodologies. Our focus here will be on *quantitative* cost risk assessment. There are qualitative risk assessment methodologies, but

---

[1] The risk terminology focuses attention on the possibility of undesirable consequences. Obviously, it is possible for uncertain desirable consequences to occur, such as an unexpected or early breakthrough in technology. This is covered explicitly in general and cost risk analysis, in that positive outcomes have nonzero probability. However, most decisionmakers want to be able to understand potential problems as their first priority, and it is a fact of life that cost overruns are much more common than underruns. In addition, with the complexity of most DoD acquisitions and the annual authorization and appropriation process for funding programs, whether a program schedule could be significantly accelerated to take advantage of positive outcomes is arguable.

the practitioners of project risk analysis and cost risk analysis are somewhat divided on their utility.[2]

Quantitative methods attempt to assign numerical values to cost increases and to the probability that those increases may occur. In contrast, qualitative methods divide both consequences and probability into a small number (three to five) of broad categories that are then characterized by numerical ranges (e.g., "0–20% probability") or phrases (e.g., "very unlikely"). For example, the development of each component of a complex project would be assessed along these two dimensions; this bivariate rating would then be passed along to a decisionmaker to help identify which components are driving most of the risk. Proponents of qualitative assessment assert that trying for more-precise quantification of probability and cost increase is meaningless in the face of substantial uncertainty. However, the qualitative methods are not as useful in aggregating lower-level risks to project-wide risk assessments, because it is not clear how to combine such broad ranges of probability and cost increase into a final, single qualitative risk assessment. In particular, since one major output of a cost risk analysis is to set the budget for a project, quantitative methods are more appropriate. Qualitative methods, however, can be valuable for providing a better understanding of individual risks and for developing a risk mitigation plan.

It is convenient for discussion to divide the approaches to quantitative cost risk assessment into two basic classes: deterministic and probabilistic. *Probabilistic* methods explicitly use probability theory to quantify uncertainty and to aggregate uncertainties from different events. *Deterministic* methods, in contrast, do not use probability theory to capture uncertainty. Instead, they compute a single numerical result from a given set of inputs; then, multiple scenarios or different contingencies are each analyzed to assess uncertainty informally.

---

[2] Hillson (1998). Galway (2004), in reviewing project risk management, cited conflicting opinions as to the utility of quantitative versus qualitative risk assessments for project cost and schedule risk.

Box 4.1. Illustrative Example: Overview

To make the discussion concrete, we use an example with simulated data and apply most of the methods to it. The example is drawn from the research on airframe costs by Resetar, Rogers, and Hess (1991). In this study, the authors used historical data to develop CERs for a variety of recurring and nonrecurring manufacturing costs as a function of empty weight and maximum speed and applied these relationships, with appropriate inputs, to the projected costs for using advanced airframe materials. For our example, we have taken these authors' CERs for recurring costs, applied them to their "Case 1" example of an all-aluminum structure, and calculated the recurring costs for 100 airframes (Resetar, Rogers, and Hess, 1991, Table 26, p. 73). We also use the same hourly rates for engineering and labor, which were reported in FY 1990 dollars (Resetar, Rogers, and Hess, 1991, p. 76). Using the input values, we arrive at recurring base estimate of $2.9 billion in FY 1990 dollars (same as their example).

Deterministic Cost Risk Methodologies

Deterministic methods use several point cost estimates for a project's cost—based on either history or varying inputs to deterministic cost models—and informally assess the uncertainty in the primary cost estimate by looking at the spread of alternative or historical estimates. The analyst provides the decisionmaker with the set of values, and the decisionmaker must then evaluate the current estimate relative to the set. One difficulty with some variants of the deterministic methods is that portraying the simultaneous effect of changes in several variables is difficult to do accurately. We examine in more detail three deterministic methodologies: historical analogies, CGFs, and sensitivity analysis.

Historical Analogies. The method of historical analogies is deceptively easy to describe: The analyst computes the projected final cost of the current project using usual cost estimation methods,

Box 4.2. Illustrative Example: Historical Method Application

We illustrate[3] one possible method of using historical analogies with the example introduced above. We have estimated the cost to manufacture the 100 airframes for the new aircraft to be $2.9 billion (median value), and we have nine "previous" programs with which to compare this estimate.[4] Assuming that all the program costs have been suitably normalized and that we have judged the previous programs to be broadly "similar" to the new one, we can see in Figure 4.1 how the new cost (the horizontal line) compares with the costs of previous projects.

Figure 4.1
Illustration of Historical Analogy

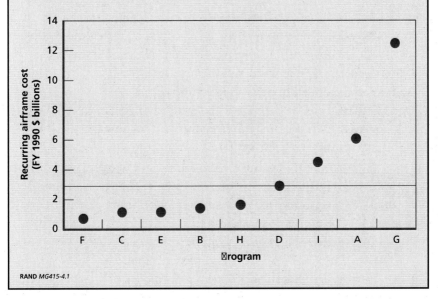

---

[3] In general, we will focus on the major characteristics of each method, not going into all the details required to use the method in a real problem.

[4] For proprietary reasons, we generated hypothetical recurring airframe costs for nine aircraft using the same CERs to serve as our historical comparison sample. The empty weight and speed characteristics for the nine were based on values for actual aircraft.

Box 4.2. (continued)

The previous program costs in Figure 4.1 have been sorted in order of cost for easy comparisons. We can see that the new program lies about one-quarter of the way from the low value of the range; we also see that the range of "previous" program costs was $635 million to $12.4 billion, which gives a decisionmaker an intuitive idea of what kind of variability might be expected in the new project. Indeed, at that point, a decisionmaker might ask why the program under consideration is expected to be so low in the range of costs if indeed all are considered representative systems.

which, when summed up for the entire project, gives a single number (point estimate). The analyst then retrieves the historical final costs of a set of similar projects and presents the entire set of numbers to the decisionmaker. The historical numbers should usually be normalized (e.g., for quantity) to provide a valid comparison.

The attractions of the historical analogy method are obvious: It is fast and easy to implement, especially with adequate data at hand. Even if data must be assembled from scratch, usually final costs for a project and even its major subsystems are relatively easy to find, especially for recent projects and those that are major acquisitions. Further, the only requirement of information for the project under consideration is whatever is required for the point estimate, which can be minimal in the early stages of development.

However, the method does require credible data. More importantly, "similar projects" can be *very* difficult to define in practice, and people may legitimately differ on which characteristics are important in defining similar and dissimilar. Recent studies that have used historical cost data (e.g., Drezner et al., 1993) divide projects into categories such as missiles, ships, and fighter aircraft. But even within these categories, substantive differences exist, or may be argued to exist, between carrier- and land-based fighters, stealth and conventional airframes, etc. In addition, the passage of time and the concomitant changes in technology make comparisons with older projects subject to objections of relevance as well. Subjective judgment in selecting the comparison projects is impossible to avoid.

Cost Growth Factors. CGFs build on the historical analogy method. In this methodology, historical cost growth of projects is analyzed by taking the ratio of final cost to initial cost estimate[5] and then using univariate statistical methods (e.g., simple linear regression) to estimate a growth rate for current similar projects. This analysis leads to an adjustment factor similar to those in Tables 2.1 and 2.2, which is applied to an estimate to modify for growth from an aggregate of factors that are not treated individually. The details for calculating CGFs have been discussed in Chapter Two. The growth factor can also provide an estimate of the uncertainty in that the historical variance of estimates can be determined and applied to the new situation.

This method has many of the characteristics of the historical analogy approach. It is fast and easy to do. While credible data are required, they are usually easy to assemble. Only a point estimate is required for the current project. The statistical analysis of the historical data to derive the growth factor and variance is straightforward. It has the additional advantage that it takes account of trends in costs that are not explicitly used in the historical analogy methodology, which at least partially addresses the objection of relevance of historical data. However, the selection of similar projects (and the choice of data to exclude from the statistical analysis) retains an element of subjectivity.

Another criticism of this method is that cost growth, based on information such as SAR data (Chapter Two), includes uncertainty of factors viewed to be beyond the control of estimators and managers and, therefore, does not truly represent estimate uncertainty. For instance, Congress may increase or decrease funding in a fiscal year as a result of other priorities, thereby extending the program. Such an

---

[5] In many studies, the cost estimate used is the initial one, but the method can be used to compare cost estimates at other project stages.

Box 4.3. Illustrative Example: Cost Factor Application

To apply this method to our example, we use a simpler version of the method and directly apply an average CGF (rather than a more complex statistical model). Although we do not have specific CGFs for airframe costs, we can use the adjusted procurement CGF data in Table 2.1 as a proxy. The average growth factor was 1.44, with a standard deviation of 0.42. Because we know that the distribution is skewed, it is better to do the analysis in logspace. The average log of the CGF is 0.317, with a standard deviation of 0.311. Applying these values to our $2.9 billion estimate, we get an adjusted point estimate (median value, not mean) of $4.0 billion with −1 standard deviation of $2.9 billion and +1 standard deviation of $5.4 billion.

---

extension would likely result in cost increase for the program. Thus, the cost growth method overstates the estimate uncertainty by including such exogenous factors. A counter to this argument is that the cost growth method represents the *funding* uncertainty and is, perhaps, more relevant to decisionmakers trying to plan budgets.

Sensitivity Analysis. Unlike the previous two deterministic methods, sensitivity analysis provides insight into the uncertainty of a cost estimate by focusing on the assumptions and nature of the cost estimation of the project under consideration. Historical data enter only as they are used in the underlying cost estimation method. In sensitivity analysis, the inputs used for cost estimation (e.g., weight, speed, power consumption, performance requirements) are systematically varied to see what effect the variation has on the final estimated cost. The goal is to see which inputs are "drivers"—that is, those that have the greatest effect on the final cost. Those drivers can then be subjected to greater scrutiny and control during development to keep changes small. Correspondingly, inputs that are not drivers of the final cost do not have to receive such attention. The methodology derives from engineering where complex but parametric relationships

Box 4.4. Illustrative Example: Sensitivity Analysis Application

For our example, the uncertainty in sensitivity analysis terms centers on the choice of inputs for the weight and the required speed. Sensitivity analysis examines how much changes in those parameters affect the cost by varying those input parameters in the regression CERs and determining how much the total cost would change. If we vary the weight by +/− 5,000 pounds or the required speed by +/− 100 knots, we find that the airframe manufacturing costs would shift as shown in Table 4.1. Essentially, the cost varies by about 30 percent by varying weights and 10 percent by varying the speed for this example.

Table 4.1
Sensitivity Analysis for Manufacturing Costs

	−	+
Weight	$2.4 billion	$3.3 billion
Speed	$2.7 billion	$3.0 billion

exist between inputs and output, although the method can be used with complex stochastic simulations as well. However, part of the uncertainty in cost estimating is that one may not know, precisely, the values for these input factors. Or these input values might change or evolve as a result of external events. Or there may be significant factors not captured in the cost estimation method(s) chosen.

Sensitivity analysis as usually practiced is deterministic because the inputs are varied over a range that is usually selected to be the minimum and maximum practical or likely values of the inputs. In particular, no formal account is taken of the probability of seeing such variation in practice. Therefore, a key driver may be identified by the method but may not be particularly variable in a specific project. In addition, the range of variation may not be easy to specify a priori, especially for those projects pushing current technology or incorporating technology where the state of the art is rapidly changing.

However, sensitivity analysis is conceptually simple to do, and therefore to explain, and the identification of key drivers is important in its own right, especially in the early stages of project formulation. For a complex project with many inputs, though, displaying the results of the analysis concisely and understandably can be difficult; however, graphics such as the tornado plot can help to organize the information. A more troublesome problem arises when significant interactions take place between inputs, such that costs increase greatly only when two or more inputs vary simultaneously. Designing and executing sensitivity analyses that detect these interactions is complex, and displaying the output can be difficult.

A variation on this technique that has been proposed by Paul Garvey (2005)—called the "scenario-based" approach[6]—is specifically tailored for cost risk analysis. For this method, an excursion(s) from the initial estimate basis is developed that includes a set of selected hazards that are of concern or that a decisionmaker wants to guard against. The resulting project cost with these risks is computed, giving the decisionmaker a view of the shift in cost over several different situations or scenarios of interest. The difference in cost between the initial cost basis and the scenario is the risk reserve needed. Using the same airframe example, suppose that we want to guard against the risk of a 5 percent growth in weight and speed based on historical understanding of weight growth over a program and the concern that a new threat might change requirements. The total cost for this new scenario would be approximately $3.1 billion. So, for our example, about $0.2 billion will be needed as a risk reserve. Garvey has also proposed an extension of this methodology for computing an approximate probability distribution for the total cost using the information from the selected scenario.

Probabilistic Cost Risk Methodologies

In contrast to deterministic methods, probabilistic approaches treat the future final cost of a project as a random variable and use formal

---

[6] See Appendix F for more detail.

probability methods to quantify its uncertainty. In particular, the ultimate goal is to estimate a cumulative distribution function (equivalently, a probability distribution function) for the final cost, which in principle contains all of the uncertainty information and allows the computation and comparison of the riskiness of different projects. Here we review five probabilistic methods: propagation of errors, expert judgment, error of estimating method, method of moments, and Monte Carlo simulation.

Propagation of Errors. The propagation of errors method is an analytic version of sensitivity analysis. It arose in the field of numerical computing, where long sequences of computations with imprecise inputs and limited accuracy gave rise to errors in the final result. The goal was therefore to try to bound those errors based on the precision of the inputs, the accuracy of the computer, and the form of the equations being used. We give a brief description here to show why in principle the method applies to uncertainty analysis.[7]

For simple addition and subtraction, errors simply add, but for more-complex operations such as multiplication, division, trigonometric functions, and so forth, more-complex formulas are needed to compute error propagation. For analytic tractability, most classical methods depend on approximations to changes in the final value due to small perturbations in the input variables. The error is a sum of individual errors weighted by partial derivatives of the functions or expressions. The sizes of the errors are given in terms of the standard deviation of their distribution. However, the errors have to be suitably small compared with the variation of the final result for the approximation to be accurate. Further, for very complex equations, taking partial derivatives may not be easy (although computer algebra programs have greatly eased this task).

One advantage of the propagation of errors method is that it does not require simulation, although like simulation it gives only an approximate answer, not an exact one. It also is well known and

---

[7] For more detailed information, see, for example, Henrici (1964).

Box 4.5. Illustrative Example: Propagation of Errors Application

To simplify the example application of this method (using the same airframe example), we focus only on the variance (error) associated with the forecast for each CER. As was seen in the prior example, uncertainty due to the inputs was small (about 3 percent), so such a simplification is reasonable. Further, we will assume that the errors for each CER are uncorrelated. The absolute variance of the sum is equal to the sum of the absolute variances to a first-order approximation using this method. Adding each of the variances and taking the square root, we arrive at an absolute standard deviation for our example of $0.99 billion, or a coefficient of variation of 0.34 (recall that the mean forecast was $2.9 billion). This compares favorably with the standard error of 0.36 (for a log model) reported by Hess and Romanoff (1987) for total airframe cost (recurring and nonrecurring).

accepted outside the cost analysis field, particularly in fields closely tied to acquisition—namely, science and engineering. However, in a large, complex cost estimation, there may be chains of complex equations (most CERs are nonlinear), meaning that doing the analytic work to compute the partial derivatives would likely be almost as complex as doing a simulation. On balance, the method does not seem to have any advantages in doing cost uncertainty computations, particularly since some of the probabilistic methods to be covered next are easier to implement.[8]

Expert Judgment. During the early stages of cost estimation, especially for technologically advanced projects, cost estimators sometimes face the situation of having little relevant data available. For example, historical data may be limited to platforms using very different technologies than the one under consideration. In this case,

---

[8] Morgan and Henrion (1990, p. 183ff) also give a brief explication of propagation of errors for uncertainty analysis, although they do not use this term. They also have much more discussion of uncertainty analysis using fully probabilistic methods.

cost estimators often turn to subject-matter experts to help subjectively estimate costs and the variability of key drivers.

This process of elicitation of probability distributions for inputs requires an expert to specify key parts of the distribution for one or more inputs. For example, the expert may be asked to give the maximum, minimum, and most likely value of the weight or power consumption of a new system. Other alternatives are to ask for the mean and variance of the distribution, or some set of selected percentiles, such as the 10th, 50th, and 90th. After these parameters are collected, either by a trained facilitator or via a paper or Web survey, probability distributions such as the normal or the triangular are fit to them to provide a complete distribution for the input in question. These probability distributions in turn can be used with other probabilities based on actual data or by themselves to quantify cost uncertainties.

Expert judgment is very flexible. It can be carried out at any level of detail, from the project itself down to different levels of the

---

Box 4.6. Illustrative Example: Expert Opinion Application

Consider again our airframe example. Instead of using the "historical" data, we might prefer simply to ask an experienced airframe industrial engineer how much recurring labor it will take to manufacture the new airframe, given its characteristics. One common elicitation practice is to take the expert's maximum and minimum estimates and make them the 90 percent and 10 percent points, respectively of the final distribution.[9] Garvey (2000, p. 194) gives some convenient formulas for computing the actual parameters of the triangle distribution in this case.

---

[9] As noted elsewhere, the empirical basis for much of elicitation practice is slim. The translation of end points to percentiles is an ad hoc practice based on the finding that it is very difficult, even for an expert, to give accurate information about the tails of a distribution. See the papers in Kahneman, Slovic, and Tversky (1982) and Garthwaite, Kadane, and O'Hagan (2004). Raymond (1999) notes that "Expert judgment is typically the crux of cost and schedule estimates, but in the spectrum of the risk management process, quantification of expert judgment is the weakest area."

WBS.[10] It can also be used for any cost-related quantities for which the expert feels comfortable expressing an uncertainty judgment: performance or physical parameters, project management quantities such as time required or possibility of unforeseen development obstacles. And, furthermore, this is applicable, as noted above, to systems that are quite different from those built to date.

However, expert judgment in such areas is subject to known biases that can impose certain inaccuracies on the probability distributions derived from the expert's inputs.[11] Further, these biases can be affected by the way in which the elicitation is done, including how questions are phrased, the order in which they are presented, and the amount and type of feedback given to the expert about the implications of the judgments made. This makes it essential that elicitations be carefully conducted and documented. This in turn means that careful elicitation of subjective probability distributions for different systems and subsystems of a complex project can be time consuming and can require substantial commitment of personnel, by both experts and elicitation facilitators.

Although some work has been done on both the psychology and implementation of elicitation,[12] little of this literature is referenced in the cost estimation literature.[13] There is also little documentation in the cost estimation literature on how to perform elicitations, as well as little assessment of how those methods can be expected to perform

---

[10] There is some controversy on the value of disaggregation. Garthwaite, Kadane, and O'Hagan (2004) point out that there is empirical evidence that separate assessments give much larger probability for a combined event than a single assessment for the combined event itself. However, Morgan and Henrion cite (1990, p. 116) that it seems to be an "article of faith" that disaggregated approach performs better for elicitation practice.

[11] See, for example, Kahnemann, Slovic, and Tversky (1982); Kadane and Wolfson (1998); and Garthwaite, Kadane, and O'Hagan (2004).

[12] Kadane and Wolfson (1998); O'Hagan (1998); and the discussion of these papers following each one. See also Garthwaite, Kadane, and O'Hagan (2004).

[13] See, for example, Wallenius (1985); Garvey (2000); and Conrow (2000). There is an empirical literature on cost estimation for software projects that looks at the performance of experts, both individually and in groups. However, this literature also has little overlap with the elicitation work cited above. See, for example, Kitchenham et al. (2002) and Pfleeger, Shepperd, and Tesoriero (2000).

in actual cost risk experience. The most typical elicitation appears to be the maximum, minimum, and most likely value assessments, which are then fit to a triangular distribution. In general, an expert gets little feedback on implications of the assessments made, nor is the process well documented in many cases.[14]

Note that the method of expert judgment in the end results in a set of probability distributions for the cost of individual parts of a project. To get the overall probability distribution for the total project cost, we would have to combine the component *distributions* using one of the other methods (e.g., Monte Carlo simulations) discussed later in this chapter.

Error of Estimating Method. Much parametric cost estimation is done using CERs—statistical regression models that are built from historical data and relate the costs of systems, subsystems, or entire projects to plausible independent variables such as weight, technical immaturity, and so forth.[15] There is substantial literature on the form of these equations and methods of estimation for different types of systems and different project stages, but one output of the statistical modeling is a probability distribution of the cost at each value of the inputs (in multiple linear regression with normal errors, for example, the estimated cost has a normal distribution with mean determined

---

Box 4.7. Illustrative Example: Error of Estimating Method Application

In our nominal example, the CERs are for components of the total cost, not for the total cost itself. Therefore, this method is not directly applicable to our example. To get the total cost distribution, we would have to combine the component *distributions* using one of the other methods discussed in this chapter (as we showed for the propagation of errors method).

---

[14] Contrast this with the view in Garthwaite, Kadane, and O'Hagan (2004).

[15] See, for example, Lee (1997); Book (2001); and Bearden (2001).

by values selected for the independent variables). It seems natural to use these cost probability distributions to quantify cost uncertainty.

The statistical techniques used to construct and interpret CERs are well developed, their assumptions and limitations are well understood, and the probability distribution captures the residual uncertainties in costs once the values of the independent variables are specified. However, the CER-derived distributions do not capture the uncertainties in the values of the independent variables themselves, which may be substantial. Further, given that the independent variables are chosen because they are key determinants of the total cost, variability in them can have an important effect on the final cost.

Obviously, developing the CER requires data, and if CERs are needed for systems and subsystems, data at that level of detail are required. As with all of the methods that rely on data, some subjective judgment is required to determine which data are relevant and should be included in the CER and which should be excluded.

Also, some technical issues with regressions come into play in the situations encountered in cost estimation and need to be understood. First, the number of data points available for fitting CERs is typically fairly small after relevant data are selected for analysis. This means that the number of independent variables that can practically be used in modeling most DoD systems or subsystems is normally limited to one or, at most, two. Further, if the value of the independent variables for the new project/system/subsystem falls outside the range of data used to estimate the CER, the probability distribution may be incorrect.[16] And for system and subsystem CERs, another method such as Monte Carlo must be used to combine the individual distributions into a distribution for the total cost.

Perhaps surprisingly, given the long and widespread use of regression models in applied science and engineering, some technical issues are currently being debated in the cost estimation community

---

[16] Regression methods usually increase the spread of the probability distribution for the dependent variable at extrapolated values of the independent variables, but there is also the possibility that the form of the regression may change outside of the original data range, rendering the estimated probability distribution seriously flawed at these values.

for CERs. Book and Young (1997) recently argued for a new regression formulation for cost estimation instead of the traditional log-linear form. These new methods have been used in Version 8 of the unmanned spacecraft model (UMSC-8) to derive the individual CERs[17] and have also been made available in cost risk tools such as ACEIT (Automated Cost Estimating Integrated Tools).[18] Somewhat surprisingly, the mainstream statistical literature has not addressed these issues in any depth.[19] So even for this methodology, technical issues remain to be resolved.

Method of Moments. The method of moments is an analytic (non-simulation) way to roll up a set of system and subsystem distributions to get a total cost probability distribution. The method is simple to describe. A set of probability distributions for individual cost elements is assembled from elicited distributions or distributions derived from CERs or historical data. Since the total cost of the project is the sum of the individual costs, the distribution of the sum of these costs is the required measure of uncertainty in the final cost. For example, if all the component distributions are normal, the distribution of the sum is proven by probability theory to be normal itself with the mean equal to the sum of the means and with variance equal to sum of the component variances, adjusted by the correlations between the component distributions, if any.[20] At this point, an analyst can use the mean, variance, and the fact that the distribution is normal to compute such quantities as percentiles of the final distribution (the median, the 80th percentile, etc.).

The addition of the means and variances holds for any reasonable distribution,[21] hence the name method of moments, because the

---

[17] USMC-8 documentation. Online at www.uscm8.com.

[18] Written by Tecolote Research Inc. Online at www.tecolote.com.

[19] A search of the Current Index to Statistics, maintained by the American Statistical Association, turned up few references to multiplicative error models. One paper, Eagleson and Muller (1997) noted that these models "occur quite frequently in applications."

[20] The form of the adjustment can be complex if there are many nonzero correlations, but it is straightforward if tedious to write out.

[21] Technically, this is any distribution that has a mean and a variance.

(first two) moments of the final distribution are determined from the moments of the component distributions. However, to use the mean and variance to compute such quantities as percentiles accurately, the analyst must know what the final distribution is.

Unfortunately, only in certain special cases, such as with normal component distributions, is the distribution of the sum exactly that of a known random variable, particularly when the component distributions mix different types of distributions. In some cases, the distribution of the sum is approximately normal, and the analyst can proceed as before, but this may be problematic with only a small number of different component distributions or a large number of component distributions when there are large correlations with a complex structure.[22]

The method is easy to implement and allows the quick roll-up of component distributions, without the necessity of doing any simulation. It results in a full distribution for the total system cost, and there is solid statistical and probability theory behind the method. However, it is subject to the technical limitations described above to move from calculating the mean and variance of the sum to computing accurate percentiles of the distribution.

This methodology was widely used in the early days of cost risk analysis, when extensive simulations were expensive in computer time.[23] It has also been used for quick approximations, for relatively simple projects with a few systems or subsystems, or as an interim methodology while more-complex ones are being developed and implemented.

---

[22] The argument that the sum of a set of distributions is approximately normal is based on the central limit theorem. However, close approximation to normality depends on both the component distributions and their number, and while versions of the theorem exist for correlated random variables, they require conditions on the correlations that may be difficult to verify. One reviewer noted that long experience in the cost analysis community has shown that distributions of total costs are often empirically very close to normal or lognormal, even when theoretical conditions are difficult to verify. See Garvey (2000, p. 286ff) for more discussion of this point.

[23] See Morgan and Henrion (1990), pp. 213–214.

The propagation of errors method described earlier is a specialized case of the method of moments approach. Whereas the propagation of error fits only the first moment of the distribution (the variance), the method of moments approach can be used to fit higher-order terms and thus better define the tails and shape of the distribution. In the case where a normal distribution is assumed, the two methods are identical. Given this similarity, an example application of this method is omitted.

Monte Carlo Simulation. Technically, "Monte Carlo" is the term in applied and computational mathematics denoting a wide variety of techniques used to approximate such quantities as integrals and sums of random variables, for which analytic, closed-form formulas are not available because of the form or complexity of the situation. In cost risk analysis, the analyst confronts a number (sometimes a large number) of cost probability distributions for systems and subsystems of a platform, error distributions for cost predictions from CERs, and probability distributions that quantify uncertainty to such CER inputs as weight and power consumption. The analyst needs to add the cost probability distributions and propagate the input uncertainties in the CERs to the uncertainty in the output predictions of the CERs to obtain an honest probability distribution for the total cost of the platform that reflects all current uncertainties.

However, as noted above, only in certain cases can the probability distribution of a sum of random variables be written down in closed form. The distributions used in cost analysis vary (normal, lognormal, beta, or Weibull), and distributions for input parameters are often given triangular form to allow for convenient elicitation from experts. The resulting distribution of the final cost may not be that of a standard, well-known random variable at all.

Fortunately, though, Monte Carlo simulation enables analysts to compute a distribution for the final cost. The analyst generates random numbers from each of the component distributions and sums them to get a sample final cost.[24] Doing this process thousands of

---

[24] This is an oversimplification to get the overall picture clear. We will soon discuss some of the technical issues that make the procedure more difficult than is stated here. Also note that

times generates a sample from the distribution of the final cost, and that sample can be used to construct an approximation to the PDF or CDF of the final cost. The goodness of the approximation depends on the number of samples, but samples in the hundreds and thousands pose few or no difficulties when using modern personal computers.

Box 4.8. Illustrative Example: Monte Carlo Application

We will continue our example by showing how Monte Carlo techniques can be used to compute cost uncertainty in the form of a distribution. To begin, we assume that we have asked one or more experts to express their uncertainty about the weight and speed of the new platform. As with expert opinion (discussed above), we assume that they have specified triangular distributions for weight and speed based on the parameters in Table 4.2.

Table 4.2
Nominal Expert Distributions on Weight and Speed

	Minimum	Most Likely	Maximum
Weight (pounds)	25,000	27,000	30,000
Speed (knots)	1,200	1,300	1,500

Given any speed and weight, we can compute predicted costs for both manufacturing labor and engineering labor using our CERs. However, those predictions are also uncertain because there are errors in the CERs themselves, which are measured by the residual variance of the model. We have also included the standard errors from the CERs in a lognormal form.

---

this assumes that any CERs used have been constructed correctly, with all the appropriate variables included.

Box 4.8. (continued)

The Monte Carlo method generates random weights and speeds of the platform from the first two distributions, computes the logarithm of manufacturing labor hours and the logarithm of engineering hours, and then adds another random number to each from the CER uncertainty (normal on the log scale). These predictions are transformed back to the hour scale, multiplied by the wage rates, and then added. This gives us one prediction for the total cost of the platform. If we do this many times, we get many different predictions of the final labor cost, which will represent the uncertainty in the final labor cost based on our uncertainty about the characteristics and about the CERs.

The CDF for the total recurring labor cost estimated from 10,000 Monte Carlo samples is shown in Figure 4.2. The final distribution has a median of $3.1 billion, a mean of $3.4 billion, and a standard deviation of $1.12 billion.

Figure 4.2
Total Cost Distribution from Monte Carlo Simulation

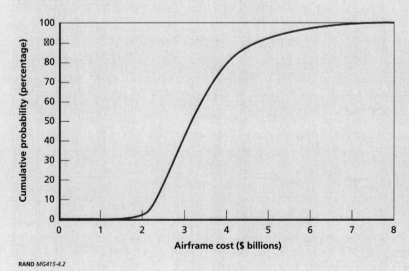

RAND MG415-4.2

The Monte Carlo approach has numerous advantages. It is a widely used, well-studied, and well-understood numerical technique with an extensive literature of its own. It can provide a final cost probability distribution directly, without the necessity of first doing a deterministic cost estimate (a cost point estimate can be derived from any desired function of the probability distribution, such as the mean, median, or mode).[25] And it can provide a cost distribution for each element of the WBS breakdown of a project that is prepared in a standard cost analysis.

However, the usability of the Monte Carlo method clearly depends on the availability of the various component distributions and how well they capture the respective uncertainties. As noted above, distributions from historical data require judgments of data relevance, and distributions elicited from experts are subject to known biases that can be hard to avoid. Further, the component costs may not be independent—that is, a high cost for one component may affect the cost of another because of shared technology or manufacturing resources. Such *correlation*—if it exists—must be captured, or the final distribution will not accurately represent the uncertainty in the final cost. Assessing such correlations is significantly harder than assessing individual component distributions (Garthwaite, Kadane, and O'Hagan, 2004).

Perhaps most important, the final cost distribution contains the effects of all the hazards considered by the analyst, weighted by their probability of occurrence. With current techniques, this makes it difficult to use the final distribution to see how well individual risks are covered. Decisionmakers in particular have argued that simply looking at the final distribution, although valuable, does not give them enough information on "what is in" the curve. We discuss further

---

[25] As noted above, a cost point estimate is a single number without any accompanying statement of uncertainty. We note that the cost analysis community is divided on whether a point estimate should be calculated in addition to a Monte Carlo simulation of uncertainty. Book (2001) has argued that the distribution should be primary, with any point estimates derived only from the distribution. Others have argued that a deterministic cost estimate be done first, and then cost risk analysis (such as Monte Carlo) used to adjust that estimate.

extensions of the Monte Carlo method that attempt to address this problem below.

Characterizing the Methodologies

One reason that so many methods have been used in cost risk analysis is that different techniques give different levels of detail about cost risk and, accordingly, have different requirements for resources: data, personnel, and time. In addition, the different techniques have different kinds of problems with communicating the results to decisionmakers. In Table 4.3, we have qualitatively summarized the characteristics of each of the methodologies reviewed above in the following terms:

- *Detail* describes the amount of information that each method can provide on cost risk. The deterministic methods tend to offer little information (with the exception of an extensive sensitivity analysis), while Monte Carlo methods give complete cumulative distribution functions of final costs by using probability distributions for inputs, expert judgment, and estimation uncertainty in CERs.
- *Time, data, and personnel* rate the basic resource requirements of each method. For time, "little" means on the order of hours or days, "moderate" is a few weeks, and "much" denotes weeks to months. Personnel requirements are "few" (one to two people), "moderate" (three to five), and "many" (six or more). Data needs are harder to categorize, but as we noted in the section above describing the method of historical analogies, this method requires only a few total costs, while a CER development typically requires subsystem costs and characteristics.
- *Communication* rates the ease of communicating the analysis rationale and results to decisionmakers. Again, presenting the results of an analysis with historical analogies is straightforward,

Table 4.
Summary of Method Characteristics

Methodology	Detail Provided	Time	Data	Personnel	Communication
Historical	Little	Little	Little	Few	Easy
Growth factor	Little	Little	Little	Few	Easy
Sensitivity analysis	Moderate	Moderate	Moderate	Moderate	Easy
Propagation of errors	Extensive	Moderate	Moderate	Few	Moderate
Expert judgment	Moderate	Much	Little	Many	Hard
Error of estimating equations	Moderate to extensive	Moderate to much	Moderate to much	Moderate	Hard
Method of moments	Moderate	Moderate	Moderate	Moderate	Hard
Monte Carlo	Extensive	Much	Extensive	Moderate	Hard

but presentation of Monte Carlo results requires that the audience have a feel for probability and some experience and comfort with acknowledging uncertainty in key decision parameters.

One point to note in Table 4.2 is that no one method dominates the others. Historical analogies are easy to use and easy to communicate, but they provide little detailed information about a proposed project beyond the total cost. The analysis can also be criticized as subjective because of the choice of comparison projects. Conversely, a full Monte Carlo analysis that uses system and subsystem CERs and expert judgment for the specification of input distributions and costs for new technology components, to determine the final cost distribution, provides great detail about cost uncertainty. However, it requires the efforts of modelers and substantive experts, substantial data, and weeks or months to execute.

Current State of Practice

The current "standard" approach to cost estimation, as presented in pedagogical literature and as practiced by major cost analysis groups that routinely do cost risk analysis, is to use CERs based on some form of regression applied to historical data to relate driver parameters to cost, either of the total project or for subcomponents or subsystems. Cost risk analysis then treats uncertainty in the inputs by Monte Carlo simulations, with the input distributions derived from elicitation sessions with technical experts or, occasionally, from historical data. The approach fits well with breaking down the project to different levels of detail to help manage the analysis and to fine-tune CER development and estimation. Steadily improving software and the wide availability of powerful desktop computers make this approach straightforward to implement in practice. It is also attractive to analysts because of its conceptual simplicity and the widespread use of simulation technology elsewhere in the business world.[26]

However, a wide range of differing implementation details belies the overarching appearance of consensus. Among these are the following:

- There are differing sources for the input distributions.
- There are differing forms of input distributions (e.g., triangular, lognormal) across different organizations, systems, and so forth, with little substantive rationale for the form chosen.
- A debate continues over the inclusion of explicit correlation in simulated quantities.[27]
- Disagreement remains about which risk factors should be included and how. Quantity changes, inflation, requirements changes, and force majeure events (natural catastrophes, strikes, etc.) have all been suggested for either inclusion or exclusion by different workers in the field.
- This approach does not easily allow for including the effect of schedule variation on costs.[28]
- Some have argued that this approach portrays an analytic rigor that is not actually justified.
- Discussion continues about how to relate point cost estimates to the cost distribution provided by probability methods. This discussion has led to efforts to determine a budget from the cost probability distribution and label the difference between that budget and the point estimate as the "risk reserve."
- Finally, whatever choices are made and used, there is little documentation in the open literature about what has been used

---

[26] In the words of one senior cost analyst, this is "simulating the project's cost" like simulating any other process.

[27] This has led to an extensive discussion in the field, notably led by Stephen Book. See Book (1999) for a summary.

[28] Most cost estimate and Monte Carlo simulation is performed at the WBS level, and the WBS does not include schedule as one of the elements. Furthermore, most CERs are based on technical or performance parameters and do not include time as a variable. (But see Garvey, 2000, for a discussion on incorporating schedule into the WBS.)

in specific cases, how accurate the methods have been overall, and for the different phases of the life cycle of completed projects where actual costs could be compared to predicted costs.

Perhaps the key problem with many of the methodologies is that decisionmakers complain that more-complex methods, which nominally should give a better, more accurate estimate of cost risk, as the results are currently presented, do not give them the information they need to make decisions. In particular, the summarization of cost uncertainty as a probability distribution, while nominally providing the required information for budget settings ("choose a probability of overrun that the decisionmaker is comfortable with, and that determines the budget"), does not provide the decisionmaker with information about *which* risks are covered, how they are covered, to what extent they are covered, and how to manage them. These are areas where a decisionmaker often has substantive knowledge about the underlying reality and wants to relate that knowledge to alternative budgets.

Not much in the published literature attempts to facilitate communication to decisionmakers using the results from Monte Carlo techniques. General practice appears to have been to supplement cost results with information from historical analogies, as well as to carry out general sensitivity analyses on known key drivers. However, three current alternative methodologies attempt to address the transparency issue more directly. The first is to allocate back the uncertainty in the final cost to individual WBS elements to reflect their individual riskiness in their individual estimated costs. There are a few different methods of doing this, including some implemented in cost risk software packages. However, none appears to be in general use, nor does there seem to be a systematic comparison of the methods in practical use that is available in the open literature.

The second method is an explicit forcing of some selected hazards into the analysis—that is, to include them as if they had occurred. One industry source indicated that he supplemented a conventional cost risk analysis with this approach at the request of senior decisionmakers who were concerned about particular problems. As noted above, Garvey (2005) has recently formulated a more systematic method of doing this.

A third alternative methodology would be to use a modification of fault trees for cost risk analysis. As noted at the beginning of the chapter, fault trees are often used to determine consequences for specific hazard occurrences by using probability calculations to estimate the likelihood of subsequent uncertain events (e.g., the probability of different failure modes given a particular originating failure of interest). They have been used, but rarely, in cost risk work, usually under the name of influence diagrams (Diekemann et al., 1996; Diekemann and Featherman, 1998). Articles written about the use of fault trees in project cost risk analysis have typically been illustrative only. Closely related, more-general techniques are now extensively used in artificial intelligence, where they have become dominant over the past decade in machine learning and reasoning with uncertain data. There is a large body of literature on these techniques, which are usually called Bayesian belief nets or Bayesian decision trees (Korb and Nicholson, 2004).

The advantage of fault tree and related methods is that using the method requires clear thinking about hazards, causes, and consequences and also an assessment of the related probabilities, all of which make the users carefully consider many different aspects of the project. Further, the tree can be used for a rigorous exploration of the cost effect of the occurrence of specific hazards, much as the method is used in conventional risk analysis. Conversely, though, building such a network may be too data intensive and time consuming for very complex projects with thousands of related tasks and subsystems. And elicitations of probabilities here as elsewhere are subject to the biases discussed above. Further, the method would probably not be useful in early stages of a project, when little detail is available.

These alternatives can help facilitate communication with decisionmakers, but it should be emphasized that other techniques may be available to work with Monte Carlo results directly. Not much research has been done in this area, and it would be desirable to keep the advantages of a probabilistic approach while making more transparent both the results and how they depend on specific hazards.

Implications for Cost Risk Policy

Overall Observations

Cost risk analysis has become an important issue because it is now recognized that cost estimates, as forecasts, have inherent uncertainty stemming from a variety of causes. The cost analysis community has conducted research on the issue for decades, with the result that there are a number of different methods for doing cost risk assessment, many of which are related to ongoing developments in the general risk assessment discipline. However, even though much work has been done in the field, technical issues remain over which there are disagreements; there are communication problems with decision-makers; and the diversity of methodologies has led to a lack of specific guidance about which methods to apply, and how to apply them, in different situations.

One further observation is that a surprising gap exists between the cost risk analysis and the general risk analysis communities, as well as between cost risk analysis and related fields such as statistics. Examination of references from key papers in cost risk shows few citations from statistics, for example, on regression methodology or from psychology on the elicitation of probability distributions from experts—both areas for which extensive literature exist. This gap is exacerbated by the fact that much of the cost risk literature appears in conference proceedings, such as from DoDCAS and the Space Systems Cost Analysis Group, which are not readily available to those outside the cost estimation community.

Key Elements of an Air Force Cost Risk Policy

It seems clear that no one methodology can meet all the needs for assessing cost risk in the Air Force's many acquisition programs. To have a useful and credible cost risk analysis, a methodology must be used that fits the level of detail required and the resources (data, time, and people) available. Each of these varies with such characteristics as where a program is in its life cycle, the size and complexity of the system, and the urgency of the decision time frame. However, it is important to focus on using quantitative risk analysis methods whenever possible, not least because one of the key outputs for acquisition cost risk analysis is information for setting budgets.

All of the methods we have discussed in this chapter need credible cost data on past projects. In the Air Force cost analysis community, it is virtually impossible to get historical data from a completed project at almost any level of detail except possibly the most aggregate. As a result, different analysts have maintained "private" sets of data in different organizations. Cost risk analysts must therefore locate relevant data for analyses and deal with discrepancies in the data available, what costs it contains and excludes, and similar issues that bedevil attempts to do reproducible analyses. It follows that standardized, centralized cost data maintenance is vital to an effective Air Force cost risk analysis policy.

Finally, the data collected for cost risk analysis should also be used to empirically validate previous cost estimates and their associated risk analyses. Such a validation would help to improve both the data quality and the estimation and risk process. It is vital to the credibility of both cost estimates and cost risk analyses to demonstrate a track record that shows how well they have done and where they have had problems. As noted above, this lack of a public, empirical record is likely part of the problem concerning skepticism about current methods.

CHAPTER FIVE
Decisionmaker Perspectives on Cost Risk Analysis

To assess what kind of risk information was provided to senior acquisition decisionmakers, what kind they wanted, and what was feasible to present to them in an accurate yet understandable way, we interviewed a wide range of personnel within DoD, in organizations that support DoD, and in other government agencies as well as academia. These interviews were conducted in a "non-attribution" mode to elicit the most frank opinions and observations possible. Thus, we use summaries and non-attributed quotes to paint the general portrait of the current risk analysis situation in DoD as perceived by senior acquisition personnel. The questions were used to guide the discussions with senior acquisition officials, although, in most interviews, discussions about issues not specifically addressed in the questions were more common. Each interview normally lasted between one and two hours, while some went as long as four. A list of those interviewed appears in Appendix B.

What Are Decisionmakers Looking For?

In general, compared with the cost and risk analysis professionals, the senior acquisition officials had a somewhat different perspective on the whole subject of cost risk, since the senior leaders must balance the inputs they get from a variety of disciplines, with the cost analysis community being only one of many. A summary of the areas of agreement appears at the end of this chapter.

Results of Interviews with Key Acquisition Decisionmakers

Below, we summarize the responses to the following questions:

1. In your view, what are the primary sources of program risk?
2. How well does cost risk analysis, as currently practiced, support your program reviews?
3. How are risk assessments currently presented to you, and how could these assessments be improved?
4. Given the regulatory and political constraints, should program risk be addressed only within the context of each program, or would a process for balancing risks across various Air Force programs be useful?
5. Should there be a set of explicit guidelines describing acceptable and unacceptable risks for programs of various phases, types, and priorities, or should these be determined on a case-by-case basis?

Question 1: In your view, what are the primary sources of program risk?

The most often mentioned sources of program risk by decisionmakers were the following:

Overall cost of a program getting set before any real analysis of the program risks is performed. For example, industry and even program advocates accept unrealistically low forecast prices early in a program life cycle, and the services focus on an objective program cost within DoD and with Congress. In addition, there is a bias in the system to be optimistic about future program costs and potential difficulties because a more realistic approach might result in a program not even getting started. Industry reinforces this bias, believing that awards are made to the low bidder and that realism in a cost-plus development program proposal will not be rewarded.

A related issue: The constraint on program estimates and funding driven by affordability within the Planning, Programming, and Budgeting System (PPBS) process. This is the tradition of "overprogramming" an entire budget with too many individual systems, all of which have inadequate dollars for unforeseen risks. When a high-priority program runs into problems and needs more funding, other programs pay the price and have their funding reduced or rephased. Thus, many programs may be affected by unstable funding and the resulting program content or schedule perturbations.

Use of OSD-directed inflation rates that do not reflect program contract inflation rates, thereby divorcing known funding requirements from availability of funding. Although not as large a problem now as in the late 1970s, when inflation rates were high and federal budgets were predicated on much lower inflation rates, many view the OSD rates as being too low compared with the actual inflation rates paid under acquisition program contracts. This results in underfunding, even with the most accurate cost estimates, which are often developed in base-year dollars and then inflated using the DoD rates for each year of the program.

Use of point estimates without including what the range of likely costs could be. This practice is driven partially by the PPBS and the congressional reporting system (SARs), which require a specific dollar amount by year for each acquisition program. Ranges of estimates are not part of anyone's thought process. Too much precision is attributed to a single number, which will inevitably be wrong anyhow.

Disconnects between requirements/capabilities generation and program management resulting in the acquisition community promising more capability than a program can afford. Requirements change throughout the development process, adding to cost and schedule. In other words, CAIV (Cost as an Independent Variable) principles are not always implemented as well as they should be.

Failure to investigate critical assumptions made about a program before key decisions. For example, there is often overoptimism about the real technical maturity of a program. In addition, overoptimism also appears in the assumptions about the level of difficulty of integrating even well-known technologies. This is often a problem with the use of what is described as commercial off-the-shelf technology that later is found to need modification to meet the requirements of the military operating environment. The decline of a strong DoD systems engineering function was mentioned as a major contributor to this problem, especially within the Air Force.

Underestimation of program complexity and schedules, especially when program advocates assert programs under review "won't be like previous programs." This situation is especially true when program advocates dismiss actual experience (historical data) concerning development schedules and costs of other, similar programs as irrelevant to their program.

Failure to ensure that the test community was "on board" early enough to determine that requirements or capabilities were "testable" at the end of the development process. In other words, requirements and capabilities were set by planners and promised by the acquisition community, but there was great difficulty in testing them during operational test and evaluation.

Faulty program cost estimates at key decision milestones. This situation is due to a variety of reasons, such as overoptimism about program assumptions, disregard of issues raised by independent cost analyses, disconnect between the program definition and the cost estimate, or failure to use or collect historical cost and schedule data from analogous programs. Historically, independent estimates have proven to be closer to actual program performance because they are generally more conservative (higher) than program office estimates.

Question 2: How well does cost risk analysis, as currently practiced, support your program reviews?

In general, the senior decisionmakers did not answer this question in either qualitative or quantitative terms, other than by acknowledging that the program cost estimates of past DoD efforts had not, at least most of the time, addressed program risks. This is evidenced by the historical cost and schedule growth experienced by DoD acquisition programs. All wanted a realistic assessment of the program risks (technical, schedule, or cost) presented to them at key decision points in the life of each program so that they could better understand the program and make informed decisions. One decisionmaker stated,

"Realistic assessments should be provided to senior leaders because program cost growth translates back into reduced credibility of the Department."

Several acknowledged that senior decisionmakers had to foster realistic risk assessments because the system tended to reward optimism and sometimes tended to "shoot the messenger" who carried bad or unpopular news. Specific improvements to the current system were addressed in Question 3.

Question 3: How are risk assessments currently presented to you, and how could these assessments be improved?

Aside from the presentation of the OSD Cost Analysis Improvement Group's (CAIG's) Independent Cost Estimate (ICE)[1] as a means of validating a program's cost estimate, program risk assessment is presented to senior decisionmakers through a wide variety of means. Most seemed satisfied with this variety; almost all felt the best presentation of program risks should be tailored to the program being reviewed, rather than being forced into a predetermined format. In general, the priority of their interest seemed to be technical risk, followed by schedule and cost risk. This is probably a result of most senior decisionmakers having a technical background and the recognition that, if the technology were wrong, the rest of the program risks would be increased. In addition, explaining a couple of program technical risks to their peers or to Congress was easier than trying to explain the outcome of a Monte Carlo simulation or another cost risk assessment method, which required much more lengthy discussions about inputs, assumptions, and so forth, and which resulted in higher funding requirements seemingly detached from specific program risks. However, most were comfortable discussing funding of programs at certain percentiles, such as the 50th or 80th percentile funding levels.

Almost all mentioned that they wanted risk assessments grounded in historical, actual results from previous programs of

---

[1] ICEs are estimates prepared independently of a program office or resource advocate as a validation of reasonableness.

similar complexity and size. The majority mentioned that the risk assessments they wanted would have to be unique because of the differences among programs. Although some felt a more standardized format for risk assessment presentations was desirable, they wanted to avoid a cookbook or checklist approach to assessing program risks, since that could result in key risks being overlooked from analyses. One decisionmaker felt at least standardizing the risk nomenclature would foster better discussions about risk. But all supported the concept of "tailoring" the risk assessments to the program at hand.

The decisionmakers, understandably, focused on "big picture" issues, feeling that if they understood the key program technical risks, the rest would follow logically. One said, "I assume the costers' numbers are correct if the technology is right, but if the technical foundation of the program is wrong, I don't believe any of the numbers." Another said, "The system needs to tell us what the real technological risk is on the program—where are the high-risk parts of the program?" The vast majority supported having an independent technical assessment performed on a program perceived as having significant risk, but these were often difficult because of workforce limitations, both in numbers of people and in qualifications. One leader stated, however, "Every program has a technical problem to solve." No one mentioned any institutional hurdles that could not be overcome if senior decisionmakers demanded realism in risk assessments presented to them.

Question 4: Given the regulatory and political constraints, should program risk be addressed only within the context of each program, or would a process for balancing risks across various Air Force programs be useful?

Included with this question was a related issue of whether setting aside risk funding within the PPBS process was desirable or feasible. Generally, since most decisionmakers understood that a point estimate would inevitably prove to be wrong when unforeseen changes occurred, there was near-universal agreement that some means of setting aside risk funding was desirable. Under current PPBS and congressional rules, some minor reprogramming of funds during the budget execution year is allowed. However, programs encountering problems and requiring additional funds must be fixed using funds appropriated for other programs. Thus, these fixes are not perceived as a true "pooling of programs" in terms of risk funding. During the Program Objective Memorandum years, funds can be moved between programs to cover estimated shortfalls with approval by the OSD staff during the program and budget reviews. However, no one had figured out a way to include visible risk funding in program documentation without its being taken during reviews. As one official stated, "If the service comptroller doesn't take it, the OSD comptroller will, and if they don't, the staffers on the Hill will." Program offices with funding set aside for risks need to hide the funding somewhere in their program documentation to protect it. Once it becomes visible, it is taken under the current PPBS process. Senior leaders felt that a change in thinking from Congress, the Office of Management and Budget, and OSD on down would be required before overt discussions of risk funding set-asides could take place. This "hide and seek" arrangement adds an element of opaqueness to the DoD acquisition process, because program personnel cannot admit to having unspecified risk funding within their program.

A new means of balancing the risk across all programs or a certain portfolio did not elicit much support from senior leadership, with most having the opinion that each program should be properly estimated with proper reserve funding available and accepted as part of the process. That would reduce funding perturbations by eliminating the need to move funds among programs to address the latest high priority need by one program that had no risk funding to begin with. This would support the funding stability that all felt was necessary for a successful acquisition process.

Question 5: Should there be a set of explicit guidelines describing acceptable and unacceptable risks for programs of various phases, types, and priorities, or should these be determined on a case-by-case basis?

As mentioned previously, there was almost universal agreement that risk assessments had to be tailored on a case-by-case basis, with a focus on technical risks as the foundation for the other program risks. Most supported guidelines on what content should be included in a risk assessment for program review, but they wanted to balance this against a potential for acquisition personnel to become too checklist or cookbook oriented and possibly overlook areas of risk not included in the guidelines. All supported the concept of "guidelines," as opposed to regulations or other specific directions, to allow program managers flexibility in presenting risk assessments and, more important, risk mitigation and management plans. This appears to be the system in place now in the Air Force, with tailored risk assessments presented to the Air Force Secretariat and the OSD staffs. One official expressed his desire to have risk nomenclature more standardized to facilitate understanding risk across programs.

Most decisionmakers expressed the need to compare risks in the program at hand with the performance on previous programs. All felt this grounding in historical "actuals" provided the most credibility to program assessments and helped contain the tendency of both government or contractor personnel to believe that they could achieve better results than did their predecessors unless they could explain specific differences in how their program was designed compared with previous efforts. Schedule risk assessments particularly lend themselves to this analysis, but cost risk could also be addressed using, for example, such metrics as cost per physical output.

One factor compounding objective risk assessments, many felt, was the turnover in personnel within DoD, both in program offices and the Pentagon staffs. With people moving every two or three years, risk assessments presented (or risks overlooked) are often forgotten, and later problems in a program often come as a surprise to successors. Most felt a robust documentation of risk assessments presented, as well as the baseline program requirements, was required to help explain cost growth in programs, especially during later phases of a program development when problems might arise.

In summary, the senior acquisition officials generally felt that

- Cost growth was due to a large number of causes, some of which were beyond the control of the acquisition community, so realistic risk assessments would not eliminate all cost growth in weapon systems

- The current system meets their needs to assess risk (since they are in a position to ask for that kind of analysis)
- Prescribing formats for risk presentations might constrain true risk discussions and that risk assessments based on historical analogous program performance was desired (where data allowed)
- More flexibility in openly addressing risk funding within the PPBS and congressional legislative processes would allow them to better address risk and decrease program cost growth
- Risk assessments should be done on a case-by-case basis, with only guidelines (as opposed to regulations or directives) as to content of the risk assessments and perhaps to a more standardized risk nomenclature.

Comparison Between Senior Acquisition Officials and Cost Risk Analysis Communities

As stated earlier, the perspectives of senior acquisition officials and cost risk analysis communities differ somewhat, with the senior acquisition officials having to integrate the inputs from many disciplines during program reviews, while the cost estimators, although dependent on other communities for inputs to their estimates, tend to focus on their products, which are objective cost estimates for the leadership. Thus, risk analyses tend to get a higher level of attention in the cost risk analysis community, which may at times be disappointed with the amount of time spent on its analyses during program reviews. However, senior decisionmakers must balance not only cost risk assessments but also all the other functional aspects of program management during the development and production of a weapon system. Unless they have backgrounds in statistics or operations research, they seem more comfortable with addressing and explaining program risks and funding within and outside DoD in an issue-oriented fashion, rather than a risk modeling context.

However, the senior decisionmakers and the cost analysis community agreed strongly in a number of areas. First, both believe that objective cost risk assessments are vital to making good acquisition decisions. Second, cost risk assessments must begin with a thorough understanding of the technical maturity and technological risk of a program. If this is not well understood, the other risks pale in comparison. Third, the most valuable risk assessments had to be based on historical data from analogous programs to lend strength to arguments with program advocates about risks. Acquisition reform and other DoD initiatives reduce program costs by not requiring contractors to submit cost and other program data; however, availability of this information in the future may be an issue. This lack of data undermines the government's ability to do a post-program evaluation to determine (1) which risks were realized, (2) how costly they were, (3) how effectively were they anticipated, and (4) whether mitigation strategies were effective. Fourth, risk assessments must be tailored to each program, which will have unique technical, schedule, or cost risks to be addressed. Thus, although the general guidelines on the content of a risk assessment can be provided, a cookbook or checklist approach could result in some risks not being addressed. Finally, senior acquisition officials are in the position to require objective risk assessments from the various acquisition communities, and there are no legislative or regulatory prohibitions from doing so. Therefore, if demanded by senior officials, robust risk analyses can be performed and presented in any format desired.

CHAPTER SIX

Communicating Cost Risk to the Decisionmakers

This chapter provides an overview of the considerations for communicating cost risk analysis results to the decisionmakers. We begin with a general overview of risk communication, then we address specifically the issues with cost risk communication, and finally we recommend an approach.

What Is Risk Communication?

Studies in risk communication have focused both on *what* risk information to present and *how* to present it. The goal of risk communication is to provide the decisionmakers with information they need to make informed decisions. The mental models methodology (used in a variety of risk communication studies and most clearly outlined in Morgan et al., 2002) addresses the former problem. It seeks to answer the following questions:

- Who is the target audience for the risk communication?
- What are their mental models of the risk at hand—that is, what do they know about the risk, what do they not know, and what are their opinions of it?
- How do these results compare to what "experts" know about the risk?
- How can communication fill those gaps in the target audience's knowledge?

This method of eliciting risk perception not only seeks to fill gaps in the target audience's knowledge but also helps "experts" and risk managers understand what concerns people, regardless of whether those concerns are grounded in science.

How to present this risk information is also important. A variety of studies[1] have focused on language and visual aspects of risk communication. For example, these studies have indicated that, to present risk information effectively to the general public, the best reading level to aim for, linguistically, is grade 8. Usually the lower the grade level, the broader the range of people who can read and understand the text. Also, the tone of voice (Connelly and Knuth, 1998) is important. A commanding tone in which the communication reads "Do this" or "Don't do that" is less effective than declarative statements such as, "If you do this, that will happen," in getting people to comply with risk advisories. Pictures and graphics are usually helpful.

Conveying risk (whether technical, programmatic, or budgetary) clearly, accurately, and unambiguously is difficult. For instance, color-coded information or other methods might be easy to understand but often do not provide enough detail on what actions the decisionmaker must avoid. For example, using a "stoplight" approach, green implies low risk and red means high risk. But low risk is not the same as no risk, and neither categorization lays out options for the decisionmaker. Even with quantitative risk data, information can be difficult to understand. For example, probability of injury might be meaningless without context or comparison points. In other words, how risky an activity is compared with another is more informative and understandable than an isolated frequency. Furthermore, how probabilities are presented can influence understanding. It is easier for people to comprehend numbers put in simpler terms (one in a thousand chance versus a probability of 0.001, despite being equivalent specifications) (Mayo and Hollander, 1991). Often, it is necessary to fill gaps in the intended audience's knowledge about the risk and deal with any misconceptions it may

---

[1] For example, see Gatson and Daniels (1988); Tinker and Silberberg (1997); Connelly and Knuth (1998); and Small et al. (2002).

have. At the same time, the presenter must acknowledge audience concerns so that he or she can better target the message in subsequent communications.

The National Research Council committee on risk perception and communication defines risk communication as an interactive process of exchange of information and opinion among individuals, groups, or institutions and not necessarily, as perceived by most, as a one-way message from the experts to an audience (National Research Council, 1989). The committee further defined the purpose of risk communication as a way to "raise the level of understanding of issues or actions for those involved and to satisfy them that they are adequately informed with the limits of available knowledge." Risk analysis entails a significant amount of information that the analyst may or may not be able to present effectively to the decisionmaker, which can cause the audience to mistrust the information presented. The committee outlined several misconceptions about risk communication. Here we present those that we judge as relevant to cost risk:

- Good risk communication does not always reduce conflict or smooth the risk management process. Decisions based on the analysis can benefit some but harm others.
- Experts and data do not necessarily smooth the communication process. Often the experts assess the same fact as having different meanings.
- It is difficult for the analyst to understand all the values, preferences, biases, and information needs of a decisionmaker.
- Finally, people differ in the degree to which they avoid or seek risk. Thus, their reaction to risk communication will differ.

Communicating Cost Risk and Uncertainty

As mentioned in the previous section, risk communication seeks to provide decisionmakers with information they need to make informed decisions. In the context of this study, that information should clearly define the implications of technical and other program risks for the total program cost. As such, communicating cost risk in a fashion that is useful to the decisionmakers has been a challenge to the cost analysis community. Often the technical and programmatic risk information is factored into the statistical uncertainty analysis of the cost estimate. As mentioned in the earlier chapters, cost analysts use uncertainty analysis to measure cost risk.

Traditionally, cost uncertainty is communicated through probability distributions—that is, the results of a Monte Carlo simulation that are presented through a PDF or a CDF, often referred to as the S-curve. As discussed previously, these methods provide the decisionmaker with the probability distribution of the confidence of an estimate. Often, decisionmakers are not trained or current in probability methods; thus, their understanding of the implied cost uncertainty may be limited. More important, as discussed in Chapter Five, the decisionmakers are interested in what they are paying for; to that end, they want to see direct links between program risks and the cost estimates before them. They are concerned about what the size of the program budgets should be and how to mitigate the risk associated with the program in general and the budget in particular. In the next section, we discuss a proposed methodology that can be adapted for various cost risk methods as well as provide much more useful data for decisionmaking.

A Recommended Approach for Communicating Cost Risk

We have two main objectives in recommending an approach for communicating cost uncertainty and ultimately the monetized quantification of program risk. The first objective is that the approach should be clear and straightforward with all the pertinent information, important in the decisionmaking, available in a single slide or figure. The second objective is that the display should remain relatively consistent, independent of the cost risk methodology used to generate the data. For instance, if only limited data are available, an analyst can rely on historical CGFs and use a display approach to bound the base estimate. However, if a considerable amount of data and resources are available, the analyst can choose to use the Monte Carlo simulation method and could use the same display method to present the level of statistical confidence of the base estimate. However, if an analyst chooses to use the scenario method, he or she could show all the major assumptions for each scenario.

A display approach used by some industry experts that may meet the decisionmakers' needs and can be used irrespective of cost risk analysis methods is a three-point range that would cover most risks and opportunities that need to be accounted for in the estimate. We will refer to this approach as the *three-point range* This approach is currently being used by the United Kingdom's Ministry of Defence to report program cost estimates. In fact, Novick and Pardee (1969) suggested that "specifying an estimate in terms of high, mid, and low points may in fact be easier for the experts to provide rather than identifying a specific value." Figure 6.1 displays an example of cost risk using the three-point range method.

Each point—low, base estimate, and high—represents an estimate with a different set of assumptions. These assumptions can

Figure 6.1
Example of a Three-Point Range Estimate

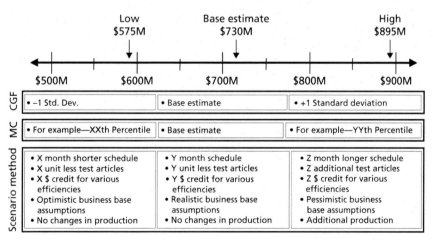

directly reflect the program's specific technical and programmatic risks and opportunities and would allow the decisionmaker to gain insight into the implications of certain risk or opportunities on program budgets. An analyst could select a single cost risk method and display the results in this fashion, but for more-significant programs, we recommend more than one cost risk method be used and displayed to provide more information. For instance, the historical cost method can communicate realistic historical cost growth of the commodity being estimated and can provide more-realistic anchors for the decisionmaker. Sensitivity analysis or scenario-based methods provide more detail of the major assumption and its effect on costs. And finally, the Monte Carlo simulation provides the level of confidence with the cost estimate by incorporating the uncertainty associated with the program assumptions and its effect on the final estimate. However, this is done at an aggregate level and cannot be easily related to a specific assumption.

Summary

This chapter provided an overview of general risk communication issues and recommendations. Further, it examined methods being used to communicate cost uncertainty. We recommend a basic three-point presentation format as a way to communicate cost uncertainty. This can be used with different cost risk assessment methods and can be easily communicated to and understood by nonexperts. The display format can also be extended beyond just the display of three points. For example, we discussed the possibility of showing a three-point range determined by a probabilistic assessment and also adding additional points to the range based on a scenario or sensitivity analysis. This combination approach gives decisionmakers a feel for potential effects of specific risks as well as the range of possible costs. The key to effective communication is that the risk information must be presented in a transparent way to address the decisionmaker's concerns.

CHAPTER SEVEN

Setting a Cost Risk Analysis Policy

In this document, we have reviewed the methods and issues relevant to cost risk analysis as part of a broader cost estimating process. We outlined the major motivation for employing cost risk analysis in Chapter Two, where we summarized the history of cost growth for major weapon systems. Our analysis focused on major DoD programs for which greater than 90 percent of their production was complete. History indicates that most programs have experienced both a significant bias toward underestimating the initial budgets and a substantial uncertainty in estimating the final cost of the system. These shortcomings indicate a need to improve cost estimating and budgeting accuracy. Many initiatives are already aimed at reducing this bias and variability; for example, one such effort is the requirement for independent estimating done by the OSD CAIG and the services' independent cost estimating organizations such as the Air Force Cost Analysis Agency, the Navy Cost Analysis Division, and the Deputy Assistant Secretary of Army for Cost and Economics. And while many have advocated for the use of cost risk analysis as part of this improvement, there is no established policy for its use or employment. This final chapter examines the issues in formulating a cost risk analysis policy.

Considerations in Generating a Cost Risk Policy

There are several compelling arguments for requiring cost risk analysis as part of the development of cost estimates. Cost risk analysis underscores the fact that cost estimates are uncertain forecasts of future spending, not exact predictions. Estimates rest on many assumptions about technical maturity, economic conditions, funding stability, operational requirements, and so forth. These assumptions are, at times, unknown or evolve during the system development phase and thus lead to uncertainty in the development of a cost estimate. Being able to characterize this uncertainty will help decisionmakers better understand (1) the funding risk they assume when deciding on budgets for future programs and (2) the relative risks when selecting among alternative courses of actions. Another benefit of cost risk analysis is not so much in the actual results of the analysis but in the information and understanding gained through its implementation. The cost risk assessment process gets estimators and technical experts to articulate areas of weakness or potential problems and their associated funding liability. These areas can then be targeted for mitigation efforts or for further investigation and refinement. Furthermore, the needed funds required to address these problems can then be set aside during the budgeting process.

Formulating a cost risk policy raises several questions, including:

- What cost risk assessment methods are appropriate?
- What risks need to be considered in performing a cost risk analysis?
- How should cost estimates and cost risk analysis results be communicated to decisionmakers?
- How should a funding level that reflects program risk be selected?

We address each of these questions in the sections below.

What Assessment Method to Use?

As described in Chapter Four, cost risk assessment methods (the quantification of uncertainty) range from the simple to implement (e.g., historical ranges) to the complex (e.g., Monte Carlo simulations). Despite the long history of cost risk analysis and the use of these techniques to assess risk in other activities, there is not a single, standard method or approach for doing cost risk assessment, nor should there be, in our view. The Monte Carlo approach is more commonly used for cost risk analysis; however, as it has been implemented, it suffers from a number of shortcomings and criticisms:

- It lacks transparency between individual risks and output uncertainty.[1]
- It is subject to subtle implementation errors that can greatly affect the results.
- It can require significantly more data and time to generate than that needed for the point estimate.

So while used more frequently, it is not the universally accepted method for cost risk assessment.

As discussed earlier, three general types of methods are commonly used and worth considering for a cost risk assessment policy. One method is to use historical cost growth as a proxy for the cost uncertainty. This method provides not only the average cost growth for past estimates but also variability in that growth. Given sufficient historical data, this method is fairly simple to implement at the total program level and can be tailored to a specific class of weapon system. One drawback of the method is that it represents only average historical risk. So programs involving new technology or having other characteristics that make cost highly uncertain (e.g., remanufacturing) may not be adequately represented by this method. Similarly, cost growth might result from reasons other than those normally attributed to estimating uncertainty. Program decisions such as changes in funding can have a significant effect on cost. Furthermore, it is an aggregate method—that is, it does not provide detail and linkage between specific program risks and the cost effects. However, this

---

[1] Some dispute this criticism, pointing out that there are methods to allocate the cost difference between any two points on the distribution back to the WBS to understand the "sources" of risk. See, for example, Book (1996). The lack of transparency is not a technical issue but more one of the presentation and analysis. The point being that some additional work to make the results more understandable is often not done.

method is easy to implement and communicate, especially when the program lacks detailed information.

Another cost risk assessment method is sensitivity analysis and a specific variant: scenario-based analysis. These methods examine how costs change when assumptions are varied and risk consequences are introduced. Again, the methods are fairly straightforward to implement. Their main advantage over the historical growth approach is that the risks can be tailored to a specific program, and a clear linkage exists between a specific risk and its effect on cost. One of the drawbacks is that defining an appropriate "scenario" or set of risks to consider as part of the change from the base estimate is somewhat subjective (i.e., an important risk might be excluded) and that a new estimate must be generated for each case.

The last set of methods, probabilistic methods, includes the Monte Carlo approach, for example. The main advantages of these methods are that many risks can be considered and weighted in the analysis and that the full uncertainty distribution is generated. Some of the drawbacks have been already listed above.

Whatever method or methods are selected as part of a cost risk policy, the trade-off between the effort needed to implement and the utility of output of the method requires consideration. That is, the cost to employ a method in terms of resources (time, people, systems, etc.) must in some way be justified by the usefulness of the insight it provides to decisionmakers. Cost risk analysis cannot be just an elegant computational exercise. It must inform the funding and management decisions.

Given the potential types of estimates needed and the circumstances, it seems unlikely that any one method or approach will be optimal. Therefore, a cost risk policy should not prescribe one method, but rather allow some flexibility so long as the decisionmakers get the information they need. For example, it will be difficult to assess cost risk for a program at an early conceptual stage (which has limited programmatic or technical definition) using the more complex methods. For such a case, a simple method (such as historical ranges) might be more appropriate and still convey the relative cost risk for the program. However, a program going through a major milestone should have sufficient detail defined to employ a probabilistic method. Another dimension to the effort—utility trade-off—must be resources and time. Given adequate time and trained analysts, it should be feasible to use one of the more complex methods. However, if a risk assessment and estimate need to be generated very rapidly, then a simpler method must be employed.

So there are two principal factors to consider in making a cost risk assessment method selection: the availability of resources (time, people, and capability) and program information (data, definition, maturity, and complexity). In Figure 7.1, we have notionally placed the three broad cost risk assessment methods in the context of these factors. Simply put, a situation with few resources or little information favors use of a simpler method. Where there are sufficient data and resources, a more complex method should be employed. There are no clear boundaries between the methods (in other words, preference for one method over another for a specific circumstance). There

Figure 7.1
Choosing Between Cost Risk Assessment Methods

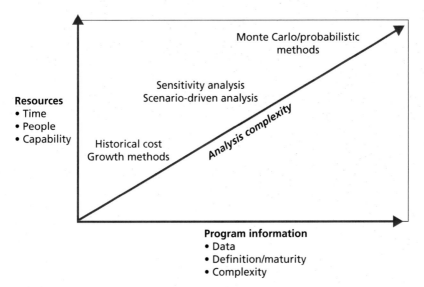

are situations where any of the methods might be appropriate. Some judgment on the part of analysts and management will be needed to select an appropriate method. The selection for a cost risk assessment method should be part of the estimate development plan. In general, we think that there should be a preference for the more complex methods (probabilistic or sensitivity) because these methods can be tailored to the program. Historical analysis should be used in cases characterized by little time or information. Historical analysis can also be used as a supplementary method (in conjunction with one of the other two methods). It should serve as the basis for a "reasonableness" test for a more complex risk assessment.

In some cases, using multiple methods might be advantageous and desirable. For example, using a historical cost growth range to set the context for a Monte Carlo analysis can help decisionmakers to understand similarities and differences between programs. It can help answer how this program's cost uncertainty compares with others we have done and whether the risk range is reasonable. Another case for which using multiple methods might be appropriate is for the probabilistic methods. Often, decisionmakers want to understand what risks drive the breadth of the cost distribution and where certain risks compare relative to one another. One approach to helping decisionmakers understand the consequences of certain risks is to use scenario-driven analysis for a few specific cases along with the probabilistic assessment. The results then can be displayed along with the probabilistic assessment and set context for regions of the distribution. In other words, the cost analyst generates an estimate in which certain risks occur and shows where on the probability distribution the estimate falls. Although this is only one potential outcome of many, it helps to illustrate what may go wrong for portions of the distribution where costs are higher than the base estimate.

Which Risks to Consider?

Another question that crops up when formulating a cost risk policy is which risks to consider as part of an analysis. In terms of policy, a desired characteristic of any risk analysis is that it is comprehensive, considering all relevant, identifiable risks and uncertainties. If an analysis is not comprehensive, factors that could drive the overall cost uncertainty might be omitted. Any resulting analysis will then under-represent the true cost risk. Although it is impossible to have a comprehensive list of risks for all programs, it is possible to identify broad areas of risk and uncertainty.[2]

Risks that are common to programs should always be considered. The following paragraphs describe these risks.

Estimating Uncertainty. The estimating methods used introduce uncertainties and risks. For example, CERs have standard errors associated with forecasts that come from them. Furthermore, CERs depend on input variables representing key characteristics of the cost element to forecast cost. The values for these input variables are based on assumptions that can be uncertain. A further example of estimating uncertainty is extrapolating beyond the range of inputs that are the basis for the CER.

Besides uncertainties due to CERs, uncertainties result from assumptions on a cost improvement/learning curve. The learning or improvement slope assumed can have a significant effect on the forecast procurement cost. Uncertainties and risks also occur as a result of assumptions of cost reduction initiatives. Often, these cost reductions are speculative. Thus, any credit given for them must be considered a cost risk until they are successfully implemented.

Economic Business Base. Another source of cost risk stems from the assumptions made concerning future economic conditions for the contractors and their suppliers. Future rates (direct wage, overhead, general and administrative costs, etc.) for doing work are often optimistic, particularly if the future business base assumptions are optimistic. The DoD inflation indexes may not be adequate to cover future changes in actual wage and material costs paid by contractors. Another economic consideration with respect to cost risk is the stability of the vendor or supplier base. However, depending on the system being acquired, the vendor base may not be stable, and key companies could potentially go out of business. Losing a crucial vendor

---

[2] In Appendix C, we outline a series of questions for analysts to consider when identifying cost risks.

might result in additional cost for a program as a result of having to find and requalify another vendor and possibly integrate that vendor's design into the system design. Even if an at-risk vendor does not go out of business, it may take additional funding to keep the vendor in a stable economic position. Mergers and acquisitions also affect the business and contractors' future rates.

Technology. Risk due to technical content is, perhaps, one of the more significant sources of cost risk for a program. Modern weapon systems often use cutting-edge technology to gain performance. But the use of such technology requires development and testing to produce a working system. Sometimes, such efforts incur problems so that more time and money are required than were initially planned. But even if the technology is an established one, there may still be development and testing issues. The use of a technology in a weapon system application might push the technology past the normal operating conditions that have been established. Furthermore, the application might represent a new integration of technologies, requiring significant development work to get a system to harness even existing technologies. Identifying and understanding technology that is new, a scale-up from that done previously, or a novel integration with other systems is central to a comprehensive cost risk assessment.

Technology has other aspects that can result in cost uncertainty. At the other end of the technological spectrum from new technology are, perhaps, commercial off-the-shelf components that can be used on weapon systems as a way to leverage commercial development. However, adapting such technologies to a military application (ruggedization, systems interface, customization, etc.) can be costly and possibly underestimated in terms of effort. Further, the life cycle of a commercial product can be short relative to that for a military one. A military system may be purchased over several years and operated over decades. In contrast, a given configuration of a commercial system might be sold over just a few years and last less than a decade. A good example of such a commercial system is computers, where continuous product improvement drives very short product life spans. Thus, ensuring a stable supply of a commercial item or technology for weapon system production and operation might require additional charges for setup, restart, or maintaining a production line.

Schedule. The risk associated with the program schedule can also contribute to the cost uncertainty. Some costs are incurred as long as the program runs (e.g., systems engineering and program management costs). So if the program runs longer than originally planned or is extended, these costs will occur for additional years, increasing the total program cost. As has been discussed under technology, development activities can also take longer than planned, resulting in increased cost not only for the development but also for potential delays to production. Another source of schedule risk can be the stability of program funding. If funding is reduced from that planned for certain fiscal years, then the schedule will need to be lengthened to complete the same technical content. While less might be spent in specific fiscal years, the overall program might cost more (extended supervision costs, low rates of production resulting in reduced productivity, higher contractor overhead rates, etc.). Yet another source of schedule risk might result if the schedule is particularly aggressive or if the system needs to be fielded rapidly. Often, additional funding is required to expedite a program (overtime costs, extra shifts, rapid delivery, etc.). To determine whether these costs are adequately captured for a program that has schedule pressure requires examination.

Other Sources of Cost Risk. A series of risks might be considered under special circumstances. If the program has content purchased from foreign vendors, a cost analyst might need to consider exchange rate risk in the overall risk assessment. Program requirements might also have some uncertainty. For example, there may be points in the development where there are planned but undefined upgrades to the system (which is typical under spiral development). Such upgrade uncertainties can lead to significant cost uncertainty. Similarly, the quantities procured can change (higher or lower), which can affect the procurement cost. Last, a program can experience unusual inflation due to the price of commodity material or labor rate changes due to renegotiated labor contracts. These risks can be difficult to analyze, particularly those for requirements. In fact, significant changes to the performance requirements might necessitate a completely different technical solution that could result in a very different estimate. Nonetheless, a cost analyst might need to consider and identify such uncertainties in evaluating and communicating cost risk.

Other, infrequent risks can affect cost. Labor strikes are one such example, which result in periods of low productivity but high costs.[3] Risks such as fire or natural disasters (the so-called force majeure conditions) can also increase program cost. Again, the infrequency and uncertain effect of such events make it difficult to assess the consequences of such risks. Therefore, we do not feel they are suitable to include in a cost risk assessment. However, both analysts and decisionmakers must understand that such risks have been excluded from the cost risk assessment.

How to Communicate Findings?

A basic three-point format is a consistent way to communicate cost uncertainty. The two main advantages of the format are that it can be used with different assessment methods and that it is easily understood by people who are not experts in cost risk analysis. The display format suggested can also be extended beyond just the display of three points. For example, we discussed the possibility of showing a three-point range determined by a probabilistic assessment and also adding additional points to the range based on a scenario or sensitivity analysis. This combination approach gives decisionmakers a feel for potential effects of specific risks as well as the range of possible costs. The key to effective communication is that the risk information must be presented in a transparent way and address all the decisionmakers' concerns.

Additional Issues

Beyond the policy, a number of other issues must be considered in implementation. Requiring cost risk analysis, although beneficial to decisionmaking, will increase the work for cost analysts. Furthermore,

---

[3] For example, see Schank et al. (2002) on the effect of a labor strike at Northrop Grumman Newport News on refuel costs for an aircraft carrier.

these analysts must be trained in the use of these methods. They also must have resources, such as analysis tools and databases, so that they can perform the evaluations. Thus, the policy will not be without its organizational and implementation costs. These organizations will need additional funding to implement the policy.

Second, it will take some time for the policy to be implemented. Therefore, initial expectations should not be that all cost estimates immediately have well-developed risk assessments. Rather, realistic targets should be set such that the organizations implementing the policy gradually increase the use of risk analysis.

Policy Considerations

Cost uncertainty analysis is an important aspect of cost estimating and is beneficial to decisionmaking. It helps decisionmakers understand not only the potential funding exposure but also the nature of risks for a particular program. The process can also aid in the development of more-realistic cost estimates by critically evaluating program assumptions and identifying technical issues. Although we do not measure or quantify the benefits in terms of effectiveness in improving decisions and cost estimating, it is axiomatic that additional information (when correctly done and presented well) is of value to the decisionmaker.

A poorly done uncertainty analysis has the potential to misinform, however. Therefore, any cost uncertainty analyses should be comprehensive and based on sound analysis and data. The analysis should consider a broad range of potential risks to a program and not just those risks that are currently the main concerns of the program office or contractor. Furthermore, the analysis should be rigorous and follow accepted practice for the particular method or methods employed. To the extent possible, independent technical evaluation should aid in the assessment of program cost assumptions.

For a cost risk analysis policy, the Air Force should consider the following:

- *A single risk assessment method should not be stipulated for all circumstances and programs.* As part of a policy, we do not think that it is prudent to dictate one specific assessment methodology. Rather, there should be some flexibility in the policy to allow use of different assessment methods. Moreover, we think that a combination of methods (e.g., using a historical range and probabilistic assessment together) might be desired.
- *A uniform communications format should be used.* Having a consistent display of information can be helpful in reducing the burden to explain results and also allows the comparison between programs. We have suggested a basic three-point format as a possible starting format. In addition, the three-point format reinforces the notion that, despite the need for a point estimate for PPBS and congressional funding processes, there is a range to a credible cost estimate, which should be kept in mind by everyone.
- *A record of cost estimate accuracy should be tracked and updated periodically.* To establish that both the cost estimating and risk analysis processes provide accurate information, estimates and assessment records should be kept and compared with final costs when those data become available. Such a process will allow organizations to identify areas where they may have difficulty estimating and sources of risk that were not adequately examined. In addition, a track to a previous estimate for the same system would be useful in documenting why cost estimates have changed since a previous milestone or other major decision point. At the end of a program, a post evaluation can be done to determine which risks actually materialized and whether their effects were anticipated correctly. This tracking process should be part of a continuous improvement effort for cost estimating.
- *The use of risk reserves should be an accepted acquisition and funding practice.* Any policy needs to provide for a risk reserve.[4]

---

[4] Nowhere in this report do we address an approach to setting a risk reserve. Some have argued for a uniform 80 percent confidence level, some the mean of the distribution, while others have developed analytic methods (e.g., Anderson, 2003). Ultimately, we feel that the

Reserves should be used to fund costs that arise from unforeseen circumstances. However, under the current DoD and congressional acquisition and budgeting process, this recommendation will be difficult to implement. Establishing an identified risk reserve involves cultural changes in the approach to risk, not regulatory or legislative changes. The only approach to including a reserve now is burying the reserve in the elements of the estimate. Although pragmatic, this approach has drawbacks. It will make it difficult to perform retrospective analysis of whether the appropriate level of reserve was set (or whether the uncertainty analysis was accurate). This approach also will make it difficult to move reserves, when needed, between elements on a large program.

---

reserve needs to be set by the decisionmaker responsible for setting funding levels. That decisionmaker should set the reserve informed by the uncertainty assessment but should not be bound by it. Depending on the program, greater or lesser reserves might be needed compared with another program.

Programs Included in the Cost Growth Analysis

Table A.1, on the following two pages, lists the various programs that were included in the analysis. For each program, an "X" indicates that some cost data were available for a particular milestone.

Table A.1
Programs Included in the Analysis, by Milestone

Program	Milestone I	II	III
A-10		X	X
A-7D			X
AAQ-11/12 (LANTIRN)		X	X
AFATDS		X	X
AGM-129A (ACM)			X
AGM-65A/B (Maverick)		X	X
AGM-65D (Maverick)		X	X
AGM-86B (ALCM)		X	X
AGM-88 (HARM)		X	X
AGM/RGM/UGM-84A (HARPOON/SLAM)		X	X
AIM-120A (AMRAAM)		X	X
AIM-54C (Phoenix)		X	X
AV-8B			X
AV-8B Remanufacture			X
B-1B		X	X
B-1B CMUP-Computer		X	X
B-1B CMUP-JDAM		X	X
B-2A Spirit			X
B/R/UGM-109 (Tomahawk)		X	X
BGM-109G (GLCM)		X	X
C-5B			X
C/MH-53D/E	X	X	X
CSRL			X
DMSP			X
DSCS III		X	X
DSP			X
E-2C			X
E-3A (AWACS)	X	X	X
E-3A (AWACS) RSIP		X	X
E-4 (AABNCP NEACP)		X	X
E-6A (TACAMO)		X	X
E-8A (JSTARS)		X	X
EF-111A		X	X
F-14A		X	X
F-14D Tomcat		X	X
F-15		X	X

Table A.1—Continued

Program	Milestone		
	I	II	III
F-16		X	X
F-5E			X
F/A-18 A/B		X	X
FAAD C2I	X	X	X
FAADS LOS-R (Avenger)			X
GPS Sat BlkI/II/IIA		X	X
IUS			X
JSIPS			X
JSTARS-CGS	X	X	X
JSTARS-GSM		X	X
JTIDS Class II TDMA		X	X
Javelin (AAWS-M)		X	X
KC-135 Re-engine			X
LGM-118A (Peacekeeper)			X
Longbow Apache-FCR		X	X
Longbow Hellfire		X	X
M-1A2 (Abrams)			X
M-2A3 (Bradley upgrade)		X	X
MGM-140A (ATACMS—Block I APAM)		X	X
Milstar Satellites			X
Milstar Terminals			X
MK-50 (TORPEDO)		X	X
MK-60 (Captor)			X
Minuteman III			X
OH-58D (AHIP)		X	X
OTH-B		X	X
S-3A		X	X
SINCGARS-V			X
SMART-T		X	X
T-45 Training System	X	X	X
TRI-TAC CNCE			X
Titan IV (CELV)		X	X
UH-60A/L		X	X
UHF Follow-On			X

List of Those Interviewed for the Project

Those who participated in the interviews on cost risk are listed below. The names and titles listed were those at the time of the interview.

U.S. Air Force

Lt. Gen. John D.W. Corley, Principal Deputy, SAF/AQ

Maj. Barry Daniel, Space and Missile Systems Center, Financial Management (SMC/FM)

Mr. Blaise Durante, SAF/AQX (Acquisition Integration)

Mr. Richard Hartley, SAF/FMC (Cost and Economics)

Mr. Jay Jordan, Air Force Cost Analysis Agency

Ms. Ann-Cecile McDermott, SAF/FMBI (Directorate of Budget Investment)

Ms. Kathy Ruffner, Aeronautical Systems Center, Financial Management (ASC/FM)

Dr. Marvin R. Sambur, Assistant Secretary of the Air Force, Acquisition (SAF/AQ)

Mr. Peter Teets, Under Secretary of the Air Force

Office of Secretary of Defense

Mr. Gary Bliss, OSD CAIG

Dr. Rick Burke, Chairman, Office of the Secretary of Defense (OSD) Cost Analysis Improvement Group (CAIG)

Mr. Russ Vogel, OSD CAIG

Other U.S. Government Officials

Mr. Don Allen, Cost Department, Naval Air Systems Command

Mr. Chris Deegan, Director of Navy Cost Analysis Division

Mr. Shishu Gupta, Intelligence Community CAIG

Mr. Joe Hamaker, National Aeronautic and Space Administration (NASA) Headquarters

Mr. Keith Robertson, National Reconnaissance Office

Mr. Jim Rose, Jet Propulsion Laboratory (JPL)/NASA

Mr. Bill Seeman, Missile Defense Agency

Mr. Bob Young, Deputy Assistant Secretary of Army, Cost and Economics

Defense Industry, Support Contractor, and University Personnel

Mr. Tim Anderson, Aerospace Corporation

Dr. Steve Book, MCR

Mr. Erik Burgess, MCR

Mr. Dick Coleman, Northrop Grumman

Mr. Jason Dechoretz, MCR

Mr. Paul Garvey, MITRE Corporation

Dr. Matt Goldberg, Congressional Budget Office

Dr. Jim Hammitt, Harvard Center for Risk Analysis (HCRA)

Dr. Ken Haninger (HCRA)

Mr. Dick Janda, Lockheed Martin

Dr. David McNicol, Institute for Defense Analyses

Dr. David Ropeik (HCRA)

Mr. Alf Smith, Tecolote

APPENDIX C

Cost Risk Questions

In this appendix, we list a series of questions for cost analysts to consider when developing a cost risk analysis.

Estimating

Cost estimating relationships (CERs) and methods
- Is the standard error (of the forecast) known?
- Does the CER include all recent observations?
- Have any observations been deleted from the regression? Does the inclusion of these observations change the estimate error?
- Are you extrapolating outside the data range?
- How well understood are the values for input factors (independent variables)? What assumptions are implicit in these input values? Do any input factors require subjective evaluation?

Learning/rate/curve assumptions
- What learning slope has been assumed, and how does it compare to similar programs?
- Is there a different break point in the learning curve compared with other programs?
- Does the learning curve flatten?

Cost reduction initiatives
- What cost reduction initiatives are planned?
- What is their likelihood of success?

- Are the initiatives independent, or do they interact (in other words, are savings double-counted or does one depend on the success of another)?
- Are the reductions independent of learning curve assumptions?

Economic/Business

How might rates—wages, overhead, general and administrative costs, etc. change due to a variety of risks (e.g., mergers and acquisition, production line move, restart, shutdown)

- How might wages and benefits increase?
- Is there a collective labor agreement(s) at the site? When was the last labor negotiation? What was the result?
- Does the program involve capital investment by the contractor? Is this investment reflected in overhead rates (depreciation, taxes, maintenance, etc.)
- Is the engineering and manufacturing location(s) established? Are local rates known and approved by a local Defense Plant Representative Office? How stable have rates been historically?
- Are there any worker/critical skills shortages?
- Are security clearances required for working on the program? If so, will there be an adequate pool of qualified workers? What costs will be incurred by processing and marinating clearances? Will special manufacturing areas need to be built? Have additional security costs been included?
- Will the workforce levels expand significantly? If so, will productivity be affected by hiring inexperienced workers?

Vendor/supplier stability

- Are any critical vendors at-risk, having financial difficulty, or considering leaving the market?
- Are there alternative vendors?
- What would be required to qualify a new vendor (time and cost)?

- What are the inflation indexes (Department of Defense [DoD], service, Office of Management and Budget)?
- Which inflation indexes are assumed?
- Are they specific to the commodity/region/labor type?

Technical

New technology issues
- Does the program use new technology or components that have to be developed or that have never been produced in a factory environment?
- Is a new manufacturing process or technique involved?
- Does a particular technology represent a scale-up or scale-down that has never been achieved (power density, number of sensors, bandwidth, etc.)?
- Are there new materials being used?
- Does the technology represent a new integration of standard systems?

Use of commercial off-the-shelf equipment
- What systems are assumed to be commercially available?
- Will these systems require modification for environment (shock, vibration, electromagnetic, etc.)?
- How long will the manufacturer support and produce the item?
- What is the cycle rate for such technology in the commercial sector? Can the design accommodate upgrades in technology?

The potential effect of new technology or unproven technology on development time, testing and evaluation, etc.
- What might be the cost to develop alternative or fallback technology?
- How might extended development and research time delay other aspects of the program?
- How many test articles are needed?
- Is the testing program sufficient (time, test articles, etc.)?

Part or technology obsolescence
- Are there technologies or equipment that will need to be replaced or upgraded over the life of the program (known as technology refresh)?
- Are there commercial derivative components (e.g., computers) that will be obsolete before the program is completed?
- Will sufficient spares be available from the vendor?
- Will a production line need to be restarted at some point to manufacture parts or spares?

Schedule

Potential for schedule delays or slippages
- Is there a master integrated schedule?
- Is the schedule networked?
- Is a critical path established?
- Is the schedule resourced (i.e., reflects need and availability for critical resources such as labor and facilities)?
- Is there any slack time for any component or subsystem that is new technology?
- What has been the typical schedule delay for similar programs?
- Does the system need to be fielded rapidly (i.e., schedule driven)?

How delays might affect cost
- Will program delays increase fixed cost, such as systems engineering/program management?
- Will expediting costs be needed?
- How might a funding reduction extend program duration?

Is there concurrent development of several schedule critical elements?

What are the multiyear assumptions?

Requirements

Have requirements for technical update (i.e., block upgrade) been established?

Is the threat well established?

If the program proceeds under a spiral development process, have the refresh and upgrade points been defined?

Are the requirements testable?

What is the risk of new or changed requirements?

Cognitive Psychology and Cost Risk Assessment

The process of cost risk assessment and, more broadly, cost estimating, requires analysts and decisionmakers to make judgments based on limited and uncertain information. These judgments can sometimes seem flawed after the fact. The field of behavioral economics offers a number of insights as to why such errors may happen and potential ways to minimize them. Behavioral economics is a field that applies cognitive psychology principles to finance and economics. It seeks to understand, among other things, why people make suboptimal choices and why people do not fit the classical economic model of seeking maximum benefit. For example, why do individuals sometimes choose investments that do not maximize return, such as investing a disproportional amount of funds in a savings account as compared with investing in higher-yield alternatives?

As a part of our objective to help the cost estimating community formulate a cost risk policy, it is important to understand the behavioral factors that underlie the decisions of cost analysts and acquisition decisionmakers.[1] The purpose of understanding cognitive psychology's role in cost risk assessment is to explore the behavioral reasons that costs, and their associated uncertainties, can be inaccurately estimated. Also, an understanding of these factors can indicate ways such inaccuracies can be avoided, minimized, or accommodated. In this appendix, we explore how behavioral factors affect judgments and subsequent decisions regarding probability and value.

---

[1] For a discussion of bias and software cost estimating, see Peeters and Dewey (2000).

Behavioral Economics in Decisionmaking

The field commonly known as behavioral economics (also known as behavioral finance) emerged in the mid-twentieth century. Behavioral economics departs from neoclassical economics in a number of important ways. It acknowledges that humans can exhibit "irrational behavior" when making quantitative choices even for their own good; in other words, people do not behave as neoclassical economic theory indicates they should.[2] Therefore, traditional economic approaches or "common sense" cannot predict how people will think or act regarding the quantitative decisions they make.

Humans do not necessarily optimize choices. They may avoid risk or seek it under different circumstances, which departs from the "rational" choice of choosing an option with the greatest expected value. For example, people tend to prefer certain sequences of gains and losses, preferring to end on a positive note even though discounting would indicate that the gains should occur earlier for maximum utility. People may also consider certain losses more acceptable than others, even if the absolute value of the loss is the same.

Behavioral economics points to three broad influences on the decision and valuation process:

- **Decision/valuation bias.** The misjudgment of risk and value arise through a number of cognitive distortions or heuristics. These biases can affect both decisionmaking and valuation. One common decision/valuation distortion is overoptimism; that is, the view that expected performance will be better than typical or average. Heuristics are rules or processes that simplify the decision and valuation process of a complex system. People often make decisions using approximations or rules of thumb rather than rigorous analysis. However, such simplifications can introduce errors into the decision and valuation process.

---

[2] In a perfectly competitive market, it is assumed that rational individuals would always seek the optimum solution to maximize profit. This rational behavior assumption is not always appropriate. See Simon (1982).

- **Framing bias.** Framing denotes that a decision or judgment can be influenced by how the information is presented to the decisionmaker or evaluator. For example, investment decisions can be affected if returns are presented in terms of gains rather than losses.
- **Market distortions.** The efficient market hypothesis assumes that pricing is rational (based on present value) and reflects all known information. There are cases in which pricing has been argued by some to have not been rational. A frequently cited example is the "dot-com" stocks in the 1990s, where the price-to-earnings ratios for these stocks were unjustifiably high, at least with the benefit of hindsight (Ofek and Richardson, 2002).

Of the three sources of distortions, the most relevant to cost estimating and risk assessment are the first two: decision/valuation and framing bias.[3] We discuss specific examples of how these distortions lead to suboptimal decisions and errors in estimating in the next section.

Review of Relevant Bias Literature

Much of the work in the field of human judgment under uncertainty emerged in the 1970s, through the research of Amos Tversky and Daniel Kahneman (who later won the 2002 Nobel Economics Prize for his work in behavioral economics). Their classic work, "Judgment Under Uncertainty: Heuristics and Biases" (1974), describes how people assess probabilities of uncertain events by relying on heuristic principles that reduce complexity to simple judgmental operations but can lead to biases. The same authors, along with Einhorn and Hogarth, have also explored how decisions are made under un-

---

[3] It can be argued that market distortions might also apply to the Air Force in terms of being overly optimistic in price expectations. However, it is not clear that the same market drivers apply with a single buyer (U.S. government) and a handful of producers. We do consider overoptimism as part of decision/valuation bias.

certainty and whether individuals have asymmetric utilities for gains and losses (Tversky and Kahneman, 1974; Einhorn and Hogarth, 1985). We describe here the key biases relevant to cost estimating that influence decisionmaking and valuation.

Anchoring and Adjustment

One heuristic that can potentially introduce bias is known as "anchoring and adjustment." This heuristic is the process by which people sometimes make estimates by starting from an initial value and making incremental changes to determine the final answer. With this heuristic, there are two ways errors can be introduced. The first is by starting with an inappropriate anchor value. The second is by making insufficient adjustments to the anchor value. Tversky and Kahneman (1974) provide an illustrative example of how this heuristic might introduce bias to estimating:

> Two groups of high school students estimated, within 5 seconds, a numerical expression that was written on the blackboard. One group estimated the product
>
> $8 \times 7 \times 6 \times 5 \times 4 \times 3 \times 2 \times 1$
>
> while another group estimated the product
>
> $1 \times 2 \times 3 \times 4 \times 5 \times 6 \times 7 \times 8$
>
> To rapidly answer such questions, people may perform a few steps of computation and estimate the product by extrapolation or adjustment. Because adjustments are typically insufficient, this procedure should lead to underestimation. Furthermore, because the result of the first few steps of multiplication (performed left to right) is higher in the descending sequence than in the ascending sequence, the former expression should be judged larger than the latter. Both predictions were confirmed. The median estimate for the ascending sequence was 512, while the median estimate for the descending sequence was 2,250. The correct answer is 40,320.

The potential for bias introduced by this heuristic has direct relevance to cost estimating and risk assessment. If an analyst had seen an initial value for the cost of a project as $100 million, for example, his or her final estimate may have been closer to that $100 million value than would have been the case if he or she had developed the estimate without that information. Thus, it is important to consider what determines potential anchor points in a cost estimate: a historical value, a close analogue, or a guess? Some anchors may be more reliable than others, and it is important to determine how reliable an estimate's particular anchor is because the final estimate may not deviate significantly from that anchor. The potential bias from this heuristic also suggests that care must be taken to isolate estimators from prior estimates if they are producing an independent check.

Similar issues arise for the estimation of uncertainty. One must be careful not to anchor experts when seeking estimates of uncertainty ranges. For example, asking an expert whether he or she thinks that a particular cost for something falls within a range X to Y might anchor the expert on the two endpoints. For the elicitation of opinions on uncertainty ranges, it is important to *not* anchor the expert to any particular values. Furthermore, estimates of uncertainty produced in a group setting could also be subject to anchoring. The first opinion expressed by one person might subsequently anchor others' estimates. Or a dominant personality might set the anchor (Pfleeger, Shepperd, and Tesoriero, 2000; Pfleeger, 2001).

Availability

Another heuristic that could potentially bias estimating and risk assessment is "availability," or familiarity; these terms are used interchangeably. This heuristic describes the tendency of humans to judge an event as more likely if they have heard about it recently or associate the event with a particularly outstanding memory. Slovic, Fischhoff, and Lichtenstein (1979) conducted experiments that showed that people tend to overestimate vastly the risk of death from plane crashes or botulism poisoning, whereas they underestimate the risk of death from car crashes or heart disease. They hypothesize that this misjudgment results because plane crashes and botulism cases are reported much more sensationally in the media, which makes them more available or familiar in people's minds. Heart disease and car crashes, being far more commonplace, are rarely reported; hence, unless the person estimating the probability of its occurrence was personally involved in the risk themselves, they tend to judge the likelihood of a risk lower than it actually is.

The heuristic of availability makes fault tree analysis, one method of risk assessment described in Chapter Three, potentially vulnerable because analysts who design the trees rely on what they know and cannot easily predict other potential incidents that could go wrong. A famous example is the 1975 Nuclear Regulatory Commission study led by Norman Rasmussen (1981), which evaluated the probability of accident, human damage, and asset damage of a nuclear power plant failure using fault tree analysis. Although the analysis was thought to be comprehensive, the fault tree did not include the incidents that led to the Three Mile Island nuclear power plant failure of 1979. Hence, Rasmussen himself pointed to the importance of finding as much relevant data as possible, thereby reducing the vulnerability of availability, when using this method.

In cost risk estimation, recent news, information, data, or prior program experience can lead analysts to emphasize or include those risks with which they are most familiar or ones where they have strong associations. Thus, in determining a final estimate, they may ignore other risks that should be more prominent in determination of cost and uncertainty. Analysts may also include parameters that are not relevant to the project at hand, because their availability heuristic tells them that such parameters have been prominent in past programs. An example might be identifying risks on a new aircraft program. An analyst might emphasize the potential risks of the avionics software based on another recent program, but the real risks lie in other technical areas, such as aircraft weight.

Ambiguity Aversion
On the whole, people tend to dislike uncertainty, and they avoid it whenever possible. This preference is clear from the experiments reported by Fox and Tversky (1995) in their work on ambiguity aver-

sion and comparative ignorance, and by Kuhn and Budescu (1996) in their work on how vagueness contributes to people's hazard risk decisions,

The study of "ambiguity aversion," however, had its roots in Ellsberg's (1961) work on how uncertainty affects people's choices in seemingly irrational ways. The "Ellsberg Paradox" posits the following scenario: Suppose there is an urn that contains 90 balls. There are red, black, and yellow balls. You know that there are 30 red balls, but do not know how many black or yellow balls there are. You must choose between two options: (a) if you draw a red ball from the urn you will receive $100, otherwise you get nothing, or (b) if you draw a black ball from the urn you will receive $100, otherwise you get nothing. Ellsberg found that people vastly prefer option (a) over (b), avoiding the ambiguity of not knowing how many black balls are actually in the urn, even though there might be many more black balls than red.

Although ambiguity aversion tends to influence decisionmaking, cost analysts might be subject to this bias as well. An analyst might prefer to report a narrower uncertainty range rather than a broad one. A broad range might be viewed as the analyst not doing his or her job well or not really knowing the "true" cost. In addition, ambiguity aversion may lead experts who provide input to the analyst to provide narrower rather than broader uncertainty ranges for the same reasons: They want to appear knowledgeable and decisive.

Overconfidence and Overoptimism
The biases of overconfidence and overoptimism under conditions of uncertainty can also lead to inaccurate cost risk estimations. A recent *Harvard Business Review* article (Lovallo and Kahneman, 2003) describes a number of real-life examples in which overoptimism has led to major financial failures for companies. Analysts and managers tend to assume "best possible" scenarios or outcomes, forgetting the numerous complications and delays that can lead to setbacks in project schedules and costs. One example the authors give is the Eurofighter effort, begun in the early 1980s by the joint efforts of the United Kingdom, Germany, Italy, and Spain. The total cost of the

program was projected at $20 billion and the date of first service at 1997. Today, after two decades of technical problems and unforeseen expenses, the Eurofighter has yet to be deployed, and the total costs have already run into the $45 billion range.

Lovallo and Kahneman (2003) attribute such business debacles not to the natural risk of investing in an uncertain project, but to executives' tendency to become easy victims of "delusional optimism rather than [relying] on a rational weighting of gains, losses, and probabilities. They overestimate benefits and underestimate costs." The authors point out, however, that not only executives fall prey to overconfidence and overoptimism, but that these are also common human traits.

However, a basis exists for overconfidence and optimism in the process of cost estimation and budgeting for projects: Every organization has a limited budget out of which new projects must be carved, and competition for this money can be intense. Hence, the analysts or managers for individual projects will jockey to present their own cost and uncertainty estimates as being more attractive (and less risky) for the organization's investment. Thus, there are large incentives to accentuate the positive in project forecasts (Lovallo and Kahneman, 2003).

Two main dangers associated with overconfidence and overoptimism are that, first, forecasts are by and large almost always overly optimistic, making the job of decisionmakers in choosing projects in which to invest highly difficult. Second, the projects chosen for investment are very likely to be the most overly optimistic ones (since they are the most attractive to the decisionmakers), leading to great disappointment for both the project and the organization.

To counteract the tendency of overoptimism, Lovallo and Kahneman recommend taking "the outside view"—imagining that one is on the outside of the project and assessing whether the cost analysts' estimates of cost and risk actually seem feasible. In experiments where this outside view was practiced, participants' final estimations became significantly less overconfident and overoptimistic.

The bias of overconfidence and overoptimism can obviously influence analysts' cost estimates and their associated uncertainties in being too low. As stated before, uncertainty ranges based on "expert" opinion may be too narrow or the downside risk (i.e., greater cost) may be underestimated. Furthermore, information provided by program offices and contractors may be similarly biased low due to optimism. In most cases, contractors' and program managers' evaluations are judged on whether they perform better than average. For example, to win a contract, a firm must be better than the others against which they compete. Similarly, managers' reviews will be judged on whether they add value by performing well.

Decisionmakers, for reasons described above, are also subject to bias. Programs need to be attractive (affordability and performance) to be funded. There is a natural tendency to be aggressive with assumptions early in a program to make the program appear attractive.

Framing Bias

The manner in which information is presented to analysts and decisionmakers can influence their view and interpretation of risk and potential bias decisions—an effect known as framing bias. In other words, people may not make rational choices because of the manner in which information is presented to them. An example of framing bias that Tversky and Kahneman (1986) cite is based on research by McNeil et al. (1982):

> Respondents were given statistical information about the outcomes of two treatments of lung cancer. The same statistics were presented to some respondents in terms of mortality rates and others in terms of survival rates. The respondents then indicated their preferred treatment. The information was presented as follows.
>
> Problem 1 (Survival frame)
>
> Surgery: Of 100 people having surgery 90 live through the post-operative period, 68 are alive at the end of the first year and 34 are alive at the end of five years.

Radiation Therapy: Of 100 people having radiation therapy all live through the treatment, 77 are alive at the end of one year and 22 are alive at the end of five years.

Problem 1 (Mortality frame)

Surgery: of 100 people having surgery 10 die during surgery or the post-operative period, 32 die by the end of the first year and 66 die by the end of five years.

Radiation Therapy: Of 100 people having radiation therapy, none die during treatment, 23 die by the end of one year and 78 die by the end of five years.

Each framing of the problem (survival or mortality frame) presents equivalent information about the treatments. Thus if people were making rational decisions, they should have an identical preference for choosing medical treatment independent of how the information is presented. However, the respondents indicated different preferences based on the framing of the choice. If the problem was presented in the survival frame, 18 percent of the respondents preferred the radiation therapy choice. The percentage rose to 44 percent (those preferring radiation therapy) when presented the problem in the mortality frame.

Framing is a bias that affects decisionmakers more than analysts. Therefore, analysts must exercise care in how they present cost uncertainty to decisionmakers. A consistent and neutral presentation of cost uncertainty will enable decisionmakers to make a more objective assessment of relative risk. This is one reason we have recommended a uniform format for cost uncertainty (see Chapter Six).

Framing, however, could also influence expert opinions or judgments of risk, depending on how information is presented. For example, suppose a cost analyst seeks an independent view of the risk associated with the use of a new material from an expert. The analyst might present the information in equivalent but different ways, such as "never used on aircraft, but used on automobiles" or "used commonly on automobiles." The framing of the technology description could bias the expert in his or her independent judgment.

Representativeness

Representativeness is a bias that is introduced through an assumption that probability or likelihood of an event or outcome is similar to another outcome based on a superficial similarity. It is the same mechanism involved when people make assessments based on stereotyping. Tversky and Kahneman (1974) identify three aspects to this type of bias:

- **Insensitivity to prior probability of outcomes.** This type of bias ignores prior or known probabilities in the judging of the likelihood of an outcome. As an example, Tversky and Kahneman asked people to judge the probability of a person being either an engineer or lawyer based on a description of the person. The respondents were also told the percentage of engineers and lawyers making up the sample. Despite the fact that the description contained no information relevant to the choice, people reported probabilities that did not correspond to the given percentages. The respondents inferred the likelihood based on the description using their stereotypes for a lawyer and engineer.
- **Insensitivity to sample size.** People will often judge outcomes based on limited information or ignore the importance of sample size. For example, one might judge a restaurant to be "good" based on a single meal eaten there. Tversky and Kahneman (1974) surveyed people on the likelihood that the average height for a sample of men was over six feet. They observed that the likelihood people assessed was independent of the sample size.
- **Misconceptions of chance.** This bias also encompasses the phenomenon known as the "gambler's fallacy." That is, people will assume that chance or random events are viewed as a "self-correcting process." For example, if black comes up several times in a row on a roulette wheel, many people will expect red to be more likely on the next spin, because it is "due"; yet the probability of it being black has not changed.

An example of representativeness bias in the acquisition realm is to believe that a new program has similar risks to another one because both are aircraft programs. In other words, suppose the avionics costs for a prior aircraft program grew significantly. One might assume that a new aircraft program would have a similar cost risk for avionics (i.e., a high likelihood of growth). However, the similarity between the programs might be judged only on the program type. Although this inference might be correct, it is based on very limited information.

It should be noted that, in parallel with this extensive set of research on bias in assessing uncertainty, there were a number of criticisms made that specifically related to *expert* judgment. First, the vast majority of the experiments were done with subjects (typically university students) who were not experts in the areas in which they were being questioned[4] and who were, in general, not familiar with probability concepts. In several attempts to make a careful study of the elicitation of truly *expert* opinion, the results were mixed. Some researchers found that experts were not subject to one or more of the common biases.[5] For example, Klein (1998) observed that experts tend to make better decisions than nonexperts, particularly under pressure. Others found that experts' performance worsened when they were then asked almanac questions in areas in which they were not experts (Mullin, 1986). A further criticism by Edwards (1975) noted that the usual testing situation was often artificial, since it typically denied the experimental subjects, whether novice or expert, the use of reference materials, computational devices, or other intellectual tools usually available when considering serious issues.[6]

---

[4] The questions used in these studies were often simple factual questions, such as the distance between two cities, and were often termed "almanac" questions.

[5] Weather forecasters are particularly good at avoiding bias. See the citation in Morgan and Henrion (1990), p. 130.

[6] Note that the expert judgments described in Mullin (1986) and in Morgan and Henrion (1990) allowed the subjects complete access to these materials.

Vulnerability of Cost Risk Assessment Methods to Psychological Biases

In Chapter Four, we introduced and described a variety of cost risk assessment methods. The implementation of each method can be influenced by the psychological biases described above. All of the risk assessment methods, to some extent, rely on interpretation by the analyst. Most of the potential for bias results from having to evaluate input factors and their corresponding uncertainties. The analyst must identify potential risks and their consequences, and possibly the range and probability of such outcomes. Therefore, bias gets introduced not through flaws in any of the methods but through bias in the assumptions and factors used in the analysis.

Expert judgment is one method of defining uncertainty of inputs that can be subject to bias. Experts—even more so than laypersons—tend to underestimate uncertainties and can be overconfident and optimistic about the accuracy of their estimates. Experts may also focus on well-known risks or those that are familiar to them (availability bias), ignoring those that are perhaps more relevant. However, Klein's research suggests that, although experts do make judgments based on experience, they are better able to recognize patterns, similarities, and anomalies. This ability allows experts to formulate better choices relative to nonexperts (Klein, 1998).

The methods that aggregate individual uncertainties, such as Monte Carlo analysis, propagation of errors, and method of moments, are all subject to many of the same flaws as expert judgment because these methods often depend on inputs based on opinion to identify component uncertainties and risks.[7] The analyst might focus on events and outcomes that are familiar, which may lead to omission of important risks for estimating the cost of a project. Even with baseline assumptions and inputs, there can be a tendency toward overconfidence and optimism.

---

[7] This is not to say that it is impossible to use historical data to define uncertainty. However, it is often the case that such data are unavailable or incomplete.

Sensitivity and scenario analysis is subject to many of the same biases as the expert judgment and aggregation methods (overconfidence and optimism, availability, etc.). The scenario analysis method may also be subject to anchoring and adjusting bias in that the method is one where a base value is adjusted higher or lower based on risks. Thus, one must be cautious that the adjustments chosen for the alternate scenarios are sufficient and not too small in magnitude, as is the tendency with this particular heuristic.

Historical analysis, error of estimate, and growth factor methods of risk assessment can be used to evaluate either component (a particular element of the estimate) uncertainty or overall uncertainty. These methods are subject to different types of biases compared with the methods described above. One such bias is "representativeness." An analyst must be cautious in applying any of these methods such that the underlying data reflect the program being evaluated. For example, the program should not be an extrapolation or technological departure from the base data of the method. The other bias is ambiguity aversion. These risk methods may be subject to the dropping or omission of observations such that the method appears more accurate. A point may be deleted from a cost estimating relationship to reduce the residual error, for example. While such omissions may not affect the base value forecast by the method, it can reduce the associated uncertainty more than is justified.

Table D.1 summarizes how bias may affect each of the risk assessment methods.

How Cost Analysts May Be Able to Reduce Bias Effects

With all of these heuristics and biases influencing the judgment of cost analysts, how can they reduce the inaccuracies that result from cost estimations? When choosing a method of cost risk assessment (Monte Carlo, expert judgment, etc.), an analyst should be aware of the potential biases associated with each risk assessment method. The biases associated with each method are discussed in part in the section

Table D.1
Methods of Cost Risk Assessment and Associated Potential Biases

Methods	Potential Biases
Expert judgment	Overconfidence and optimism could lead experts to underestimate uncertainties and to be overly optimistic about their base values. The heuristic of availability could lead to omission of risks or emphasis of ones that are not relevant.
Historical analysis, growth factors, and error of estimate	Historical data may not be representative of the current program. Outliers may be dismissed through ambiguity aversion, leading to low uncertainty.
Monte Carlo analysis, method of moments, and propagation of errors	These methods do not introduce bias; rather, the input values and factors that the methods use may be biased. See expert judgment, error of estimate, and historical analysis.
Fault tree analysis	Analysts could rely too heavily on circumstances they already know could happen (availability) and omit uncertainties about new potential circumstances that affect cost.
Scenario analysis	Heuristic of anchoring and adjustment and the bias of optimism could influence the choice of the alternate cases, resulting in too narrow of an uncertainty range.

above and are summarized in Table D.1. By doing this, analysts can gain an awareness of the potential pitfalls associated with their method(s) of choice, and they can strive to avoid the effects of those pitfalls by compensating accordingly.

One way to compensate is by careful study of the historical data available on past projects—ideally those that are similar to the one for which they are making an estimate. Historical data can give insights as to the actual cost and size of uncertainties in past programs. By comparing what the costs and uncertainties really were with what analysts of the past had predicted them to be, cost analysts can also derive a clearer picture of whether estimates have been historically too high, too low, or too tightly bounded. In addition, historical data can show which specific parameters in past cost and uncertainty estimates were too high or too low. If analysts see trends in any of the above, they can learn from history and make efforts not to repeat the same mistakes.

A potential pitfall associated with historical analysis, however, is that historical data may not be representative of the specific program or project in question. This dissimilarity is particularly true with novel programs that can be so different from any program preceding them that historical analysis could potentially introduce representativeness bias into the analysis. Thus, the cost analyst should be alert to situations where the technology for a program is profoundly different and use historical data cautiously.

To counter overoptimism and overconfidence, analysts should assume average performance and productivity. Many programs have aggressive targets and goals as a way to motivate team members and contractors.[8] However, such targets may not be easily met. Assuming that such targets are the "expected" performance could skew the cost risk assessment low. An analyst must be aware of how such goals might be aggressive and adjust them accordingly as part of the estimating and risk assessment process.

Also, an analyst should identify and question all the key assumptions that form the basis for the estimate. For example, is the assumed schedule reasonable? Do the production assumptions include reasonable levels of learning and productivity gains? Do the development plans include adequate test hours and test units? Are the assumptions for code reuse reasonable based on prior experience? By questioning certain assumptions, the cost analyst can gain insight into potential risks for the program that may normally go unidentified or can highlight areas of overoptimism.[9]

Another way to identify possible bias is to use teams to produce or review estimates. This approach may help to reduce availability bias because individuals will have different experiences and exposures

---

[8] More correctly, assumptions on performance and productivity for a cost risk analysis should be represented by distributions. However, in going to a point estimate or budget, a specific value must be selected. The values chosen from the distribution are typically optimistic.

[9] In Appendix C, we outline a series of questions probing at underlying assumptions in estimates. See also Pfleeger, Wu, and Lewis (2005).

to risk. In a group setting, multiple points of view can be discussed and a more complete identification of risks can likely be made.

Last, another way to avoid potential bias is by careful elicitation of information from experts. Analysts should avoid leading questions or presenting information that might frame or anchor the expert to a particular value or range.

Behavioral Factors That May Bias How DoD Decisionmakers Respond to Cost Risk Estimates

How DoD decisionmakers respond to cost risk estimates is not always under the control of the cost analysts; however, it may be useful for analysts to understand how decisionmakers will react to the cost information presented to them.

Cost decisionmakers are likely to be susceptible to the same sorts of heuristics and biases that can affect cost analysts. For example, their aversion to ambiguity may lead them to prefer point estimates rather than cost ranges and to prefer small rather than large ranges. This aversion is particularly acute when decisionmakers are accustomed to a point estimate and, indeed, must budget to a single value. As discussed above, this can lead to projects with overly optimistic and overconfident estimates being chosen over those projects that have a more careful or comprehensive analysis of uncertainty and true cost, which may in the end lead to disappointment and suboptimal investment of resources.

Tied in with ambiguity aversion in this case, overconfidence and optimism may affect decisionmakers in the same way they affect analysts: Decisionmakers believe that projects with aggressive goals of cost, uncertainty, and schedule could be accomplished and, hence, approve investment in such projects.

The heuristic of availability may mean that decisionmakers find presentations that include analogies to similar, past programs to be more appealing. In some ways, this heuristic works for the better of the project investment choices, because it means that those estimates that are presented with a link to historical analysis may have an improved chance of receiving funding. Further, analogies are often easier to understand than other approaches where the internal workings are hidden (e.g., Monte Carlo simulation). However, the availability heuristic may lead decisionmakers to distrust presentations of very new programs with few or no historical analogies. Such distrust may lead to rejection of novel technologies or products that may actually prove extremely valuable.

How Decisionmakers May Be Able to Reduce Bias Effects

How can cost decisionmakers reduce the potential effects of these judgmental biases? Again we offer two recommendations. The first is the same as to the analysts: Decisionmakers should understand the historical context of past projects to get a better understanding of cost and schedules risk. Historical data may help them to accept more easily analysts' presentations of large uncertainty bounds (to combat the preference for ambiguity aversion). The data may also help decisionmakers spot potentially egregious underestimates of cost or uncertainty; data can provide a "reality check" for overly optimistic or overconfident project cost estimates. Finally, historical data may even help with novel programs by aiding in predictions of uncertainties in cost and schedule. Again, however, historical numbers can also have the potential to bias decisionmakers' judgments on how much a current program should cost, particularly if the program is new and has no appropriate analogy to any programs that preceded it. So here, too, decisionmakers should be cautious with the historical approach.

The second recommendation is that decisionmakers should "redefine rigor in praise of uncertainty" (Bratvold, Begg, and Campbell, 2002). Rigor is not, after all, found in point estimates, or in selecting one "right" vision of the future. Rather, rigor requires accurately defined uncertainty estimates, large though they may be, and preparation for multiple futures of a project. To give decisionmakers such a redefinition would help them to make optimal investments in the face of choosing among many potential projects to fund.

Summary

The principles underlying behavioral economics and cognitive psychology do identify how cost analysts and decisionmakers can improve cost and uncertainty estimation. Judgmental biases and heuristics can lead to variations from the actual uncertainty associated with projects. Thus, analysts and decisionmakers need to be aware of these behavioral biases when they make their decisions, particularly in making estimations regarding uncertainty.

Reliance on historical data can provide an excellent reality check, but it is not enough. Analysts and decisionmakers must become aware of the types of biases to which they may be subject and work to overcome those biases to reduce cost risk. Assuming average performance as the expected outcome and using groups or teams to review analysis are additional ways that bias can be reduced.

Risk Management for a Collection of Programs

Another relevant question for the Air Force is what happens when considering the cost risk of a group of programs of various sizes, maturities, and risks.[1] Such a grouping could consist of a "portfolio" of related programs overseen by a program executive officer or projects assigned to a program director.

As discussed in the preceding sections, the total cost at some confidence level for a single program is not a simple summation of the estimates of the individual cost elements at the same confidence level. Similarly, for a group of programs, each having its own cost probability distributions, the aggregate cost probability distribution of the group is not a simple summation of the corresponding individual program estimates. The effects of diversification have implications for the size of the portfolio risk reserve required for a given confidence level. The potential advantages, disadvantages, and feasibility of managing risk for a group of programs in an integrated fashion are the issues examined in this appendix.

---

[1] By group, we mean a collection of acquisition programs and make no distinction for type or selection. This approach differs from the grouping done for investments where groups are deliberately formed from a diversified set of options (through either different business sectors or investment types). For our discussion, the analogy to the insurance industry is more appropriate. Given a set of programs (a group), what level of risk reserve is appropriate?

Portfolio Theory

Portfolio theory addresses the optimization of expected return from a group of assets for a given level of risk. In the early 1950s, Markowitz (1952; 1999) and Roy (1952) developed theoretical underpinnings for identifying the group of most "efficient" portfolios using the expected return (mean) and risk (variance and covariance) as metrics. Basically, they postulated that, while the expected return of the group is simply the weighted average of the expected returns of each of the assets, the variability (uncertainty) is a function of both the variability of the individual assets and their correlation with each other. Their work quantified the effect of diversification on portfolio performance. Markowitz (1999) later showed the effect of correlation between the individual investments on the effectiveness of diversification in the portfolio.

Although portfolio theory was developed to describe and guide investor behavior, its principles can be applied to any system whose behavior can be modeled as a group of random variables. Its key mechanism is a reduction in the net variability of the group through diversification. The benefits of diversification exist to the degree that component activities have variations that tend to offset each other. This obviously depends on their correlation or covariance with each other (Markowitz, 1999). (In the limiting case, if all activities have perfect positive correlation, there will be no reduction in the group variability, regardless of the number of activities included in the group.) This effect of offsetting variations within a group is the principle underlying insurance.

Effects of a Risk Reserve Pool

In applying these principles to a "portfolio" of defense acquisition programs, one would need to create a "pooled" reserve of funds from each of the portfolio programs under the control of a single senior acquisition manager, such as the program executive officer or service acquisition executive. (A pooled reserve indicates that the funds could be used on any portfolio program as needed.) This approach could potentially reduce the total amount of risk reserve required for a given level of portfolio risk because of the effect of offsetting variations discussed above.

To assess the rough magnitude of these savings, we constructed Monte Carlo simulations to compare total risk reserves required for a given confidence level using either individual program risk reserves or a pooled portfolio reserve. We assumed five hypothetical programs with various lognormal cost probability distributions; groups of programs with a variety of distribution parameters were tried. Figure E.1 illustrates a representative set of cost probability distributions. Table E.1 shows that, for the five programs, with the parameters listed, pooling the program reserves would save 9.2 percent over maintaining individual reserves at the same level of confidence.

Figure E.1
Cost Probability Distributions for a Hypothetical Portfolio of Programs

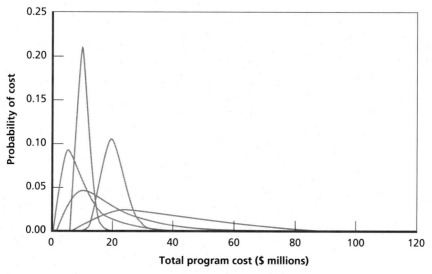

Table E.1
Comparison of Individual and Pooled Reserves for the Hypothetical Portfolio

	Individual Reserves	Pooled Reserves
Program means	10,10,40,20,20	10,10,40,20,20
Program coefficients of variation[a]	0.8,0.2,0.6,0.2,0.8	0.8,0.2,0.6,0.2,0.8
Total cost for given year (80% confidence level)	$131.8	$119.6
Difference		−$12.2 (9.2%)

[a]Coefficient of variation is defined as the standard deviation divided by the mean.

The savings over the various cases ranged from 7 to 11 percent with pooled reserves. These results depend on the following assumptions:

- The program cost probability distributions are uncorrelated.
- The estimate confidence levels are accurately assessed.
- The contractors and program managers have incentives not to spend the reserves.
- The risk reserves are available to the program when needed.

The potential savings are reduced to the extent that these assumptions are violated. If the programs are perfectly positively correlated, the individual and pooled cases are equivalent.

Since there are certain practical problems in creating a multiprogram risk reserve pool, which are discussed below, an alternative risk reserve strategy is to withhold a risk reserve for each program at the program executive officer or program director level. While this approach does not fully realize the savings of a risk pool because of potential correlations among the activities, it could be argued that this approach would provide incentives to project or cost account managers not to spend all allocated funding.

Applicability to Defense Programs

Unlike managing an investment portfolio, in government acquisition there are many considerations other than maximizing expected financial return subject to acceptable levels of risk. Public-sector procurements must satisfy many constituencies and criteria that are implemented by a variety of laws, regulations, and administrative processes. Any attempt to change the way government programs are approved, funded, and managed must take these into account.

In many government-funded activities, there are considerations and constraints not typically found in the commercial world. Some are intentional, such as a procurement process that is generally open to all qualified bidders, with the contract awarded to the offeror(s) who most closely meets published evaluation criteria. Despite the additional time and effort that this requires, an important criterion is that the process be seen as fair and objective by all parties. However, the resources required to submit and evaluate proposals and award contracts, along with the relatively high start-up cost of developing or producing defense systems, make changing contractors after a program is well under way relatively difficult. This leads to the unintended consequence that a pragmatic bidder may be motivated to take considerable risks in the proposal phase to ensure winning the contract and avoiding exclusion from the market for the duration of the program's development and production. Although the contractor will generally share in the negative consequences of this behavior, the government customer must ultimately face the choice of attempting to force the contractor to live within an unrealistically low budget, to reduce the system performance or program content, or to attempt to find additional funding, often putting otherwise healthy programs at risk. To protect against this situation, the government must not only compare offers based on price and features proposed, but also on the realism of the cost, schedule, and technical approach proposed.

The use of portfolio management techniques offers both potential benefits and difficulties within this environment. These are discussed in the two following sections.

Advantages of Managing Programs as a Portfolio

Managing program risk reserves at the portfolio level rather than within each program offers several advantages. As discussed above, the characteristics of the DoD acquisition process can, in some cases, encourage contractors to submit unrealistically optimistic bids on competitive awards. Once the contract is awarded, any programmed funding above the winning contractor's bid amount is vulnerable to being reallocated to other service, OSD, or congressional priorities. It is very disruptive if it later becomes apparent that the "excess" funding was in fact needed to execute the program. From the government's perspective, this can lead to a variety of undesirable consequences. The program schedule may slip, the contract scope may have to be renegotiated, the contractor may have to take high-risk actions internally to attempt to live within the unrealistically low bid, or funding may have to be taken from other healthy activities or programs. For all these reasons, program managers will attempt to maintain healthy risk reserves to apply as needed within the program. If the program risk reserve is controlled by an official above the program manager, the contractor can no longer count on the program manager having access to additional funding within the program. Therefore, both the contractor and the program manager would have even stronger motivation to ensure that bids are realistic and to manage according to the approved program budget.

In theory, placing control of risk reserves at a higher level in the organization should make it more likely that they will be used for higher-level priorities. To the extent emerging problems can be covered by using the risk reserve, it should also reduce the disruption of taking funding from other programs.

A key consideration in designing such a process is to ensure that, when required, risk reserves can be made available in a timely manner to programs with a bona fide need, without the delays or risks associated with reprogramming. This could encourage program managers, in conjunction with the reserve custodian, to set challenging targets without having occasional problems jeopardize the overall health of the program.

Finally, as discussed in the previous section, *if* the reserves for several programs are pooled, the risk reserve needed for a given confidence level can be slightly reduced.

Disadvantages of Managing Programs as a Portfolio

One significant disadvantage of retaining a risk reserve at a level above the program manager is the potential reduction in program manager commitment and accountability. Many recent management policy initiatives have had as their objective to increase both the authority and accountability of the program manager. Implicit in these changes is the assumption that the program manager is in the best position to determine program priorities and to judge how best to achieve program objectives. To accomplish this, the program manager may need the flexibility to invest in avoiding foreseeable problems rather than waiting until they become obvious enough to justify to external officials the need for reserve funds.

Another drawback of pooling several programs' reserves is that a serious problem on a large (or strongly supported program) could exhaust the reserves for all. In some circumstances, this could happen before the full extent of the problems is known, and the reserve could be spent without either fully solving the original problem or triggering the level of review that would be otherwise warranted.

Other potential issues with a centrally managed reserve are the continuing perception that the reserve is actually a "slush fund" to compensate for poor management or to fund discretionary activities and that the point estimate (or contract price) is the "real" number.

Finally, an identified "reserve" is always vulnerable to being applied to other unfunded priorities. Even if service-level decisionmakers intend to protect approved risk reserves, other OSD and congressional priorities and emerging "fact-of-life" demands within the service often leave few attractive alternatives.

Some Practical Considerations

In addition to the advantages and disadvantages of pooling risk reserves outside the program, some practical issues related to the DoD budget process must be considered in implementing such an approach.

The first is that, although program budgets are planned five to six years into the future in the Future Years Defense Program and DoD has adopted a two-year budget cycle internally, Congress continues to authorize and appropriate annually. Program development activities are funded only in one-year increments. With few exceptions, Congress also funds procurement one annual buy at a time.[2]

Additional restrictions on the funding provided to the program manager are that it must be obligated within two years for research, development, test, and evaluation (RDT&E) and three years for most types of procurement. If the funding is not obligated within this period, it "expires" for the purposes of new obligations.[3] To avoid losing expiring unobligated funding, program managers must continually monitor the obligation status and forecast for all program funding. Obviously this makes retention of unobligated risk reserves a problem.

A more serious problem with attempting to create a "pooled" reserve is that funding is authorized and appropriated by Congress for specific purposes. Transferring funding from one RDT&E program element or procurement line item to another is called reprogramming. There are specific guidelines for reprogramming, depending on the amount and appropriation involved. In general, OSD can authorize reprogramming below $4 million in RDT&E and $10 million in procurement within a given year's appropriation. Amounts greater than these require what is termed "above threshold" repro-

---

[2] Exceptions to the authorization and funding of only the current year's procurement quantity are congressionally approved multiyear procurements and certain components with unusually long lead times.

[3] Funding that has passed its expiration date for new obligations can be used for within scope cost growth such as indirect rate increases and settlement of claims under the original obligation (U.S. Department of Defense, 2002).

gramming authorization by Congress. In addition, funds may not be reprogrammed without congressional authorization in the following cases:

- Congress has explicitly denied or reduced funding.
- For starting new programs.
- A series of below threshold reprogrammings that together exceed the internal reprogramming threshold (U.S. Department of Defense, 2002).

Obviously, reprogramming takes time. Above-threshold reprogramming actions can rarely be completed before May (nine months into the fiscal year). However, reprogramming has an even greater drawback. Since reprogramming is a shift of existing funding from one program element to another, both source and recipient must be identified in the reprogramming request. In the highly competitive DoD budget environment, identifying funds as candidates for reprogramming may make them vulnerable to offset budget shortfalls other than those of the intended recipient. Thus, identifying funding for reprogramming may result in the loss of donor funds without solving the original shortfall.

A Previous Attempt

In the early 1970s, the Army was struggling to get cost growth in development programs under control. It recognized that its program estimates, which were largely based on adding lower-level estimates of planned activities (today called bottom-up or engineering build-up), made no allowance for a realistic level of problems or omitted scope. As a result, cost growth in the range of 50 to 100 percent was not unusual. In 1974, Norman Augustine, the Assistant Secretary of the Army for Research and Development, directed that "a Total Risk Assessing Cost Estimate (TRACE) be generated for all future development programs and used as a basis for justifying those programs.

The TRACE estimate is defined as one having a 50:50 chance of producing either an overrun or an underrun" (Augustine, 1974, p. 2).

Implementation of this concept represented an early attempt to apply the principles of risk analysis to DoD budgeting, albeit only to the 50 percent confidence level. The risk reserve was programmed as part of the program budget submission but was held at the level equivalent to today's service acquisition executive. The original implementing guidance directed that the target for releasing reserved funds to the program manager be within four days of receiving the request. In practice, the delay averaged 21 days (Howard, 1978). The risk reserve was intended for contingencies that were not included in the original estimate but were within the original scope of the program. Requirements changes, congressional reductions, or inflation adjustments were not considered appropriate uses for TRACE funds (U.S. Army, 1986).

When TRACE was first implemented, the withhold was programmed only in the final year of program development. In this way, it was felt that if the withhold were needed, specific justification could be provided to Congress in the budget request for that year. If it were not needed at the end of development, it would simply be dropped from that year's funding request. This approach proved to be ineffective in practice and was modified by including an appropriate portion of the risk reserve in each year's budget request. If the funds were not used in the first year of availability, they would be reprogrammed for other Army requirements in the following quarter to avoid expiration, unless the program manager demonstrated a valid near-term requirement for them.

The TRACE initiative was an early attempt to recognize risk explicitly and to budget for expected cost growth. It provided an impetus for developing methodologies to quantify program risk, including probabilistic network analysis. It was well supported by the service headquarters–level decisionmakers and the budget community, who felt that it helped reduce overly optimistic program cost projections that resulted in the chronic mismatch of program requirements with available funding. It was not welcomed by most program managers, particularly during the initial implementation when the TRACE withholds were taken out of existing program funding (Venzke, 1977). Additionally, it was found that, although the withholds for each program could be changed only with authorization from the Deputy Chief of Staff for Research, Development, and Acquisition, when budget shortfalls dictated either cutting program budgets or decrementing the TRACE withholds, the withholds usually lost. TRACE was eventually phased out in favor of incorporating risk reserves directly into the program budget. It is also significant to note that TRACE was never a "pooled" reserve as discussed above. The intention was to require planning and budgeting for risk on a program-by-program basis. The benefit of diversifying risk among multiple programs was never possible, since program funds could not be commingled without formal reprogramming.

Conclusions

Although there are advantages to managing program cost risk at the "portfolio" level, there are substantial obstacles to doing so within the current Planning, Programming, and Budgeting System framework. Some of these obstacles involve administrative procedures designed to provide various officials with insight into and control over the use of appropriated funding.

A more fundamental challenge is the competitive, generally zero-sum nature of the DoD budget process. Despite the best intentions of all parties, little evidence suggests that identified external risk reserves would survive except within more-protected environments, such as a directorate controlling multiple projects under a single program element or a program for which Congress has explicitly provided funding flexibility in the appropriating legislation.

Without changes to this environment, risk management of the Air Force portfolio of programs will, in all likelihood, continue to be done on a case-by-case basis by decisionmakers. However, to consider risk, even at this level, requires accurate analyses of the cost and risk for each program.

The Scenario-Based Method Applied to Three-Point Range

Overview

The scenario-based method (SBM) is a deterministic technique for performing cost risk analysis.[1] This approach uses a well-defined set of alternative technical and/or programmatic assumptions (called a scenario) to define a potential alternative program cost. The difference in cost between the scenario and the baseline cost (i.e., the estimated cost without considering risk) is a measure of cost risk. An advantage of the SBM is the causal link between changes in technical or programmatic conditions and changes in cost. Thus, the SBM results in a measure of cost risk that is directly traceable to specific conditions and therefore readily understood. In other words, we know exactly what conditions might cause cost risk and have a traceable quantification scheme to measure that risk. Another advantage of the method is that it is generally easy to implement given that a cost model for a program has already been developed. Different scenarios can be hypothesized, specified, and evaluated with the SBM. By examining multiple scenarios, the cost analyst can gain insights into the robustness of the anticipated cost and the effects of differing technical and programmatic assumptions.

As described in Chapter Four, the SBM is a refinement of a more general method of sensitivity analysis. With both SBM and sensitivity analysis, the cost analyst specifies alternative values for a set of

---

[1] The scenario-based method was developed in 2003 by Paul R. Garvey, Chief Scientist, Center for Acquisition and Systems Analysis, MITRE Corporation.

cost-related variables (e.g., input variables to a cost estimating relationship) and computes a revised cost via a defined estimating technique. To perform cost risk analysis with the sensitivity analysis method, the values of one or more of the cost-related variables are varied to measure the changes in cost. With the SBM, however, the cost analyst specifies alternative sets of technical and programmatic assumptions—each set of which defines a specific scenario. When the cost for a scenario is evaluated, the cost analyst must assess the changes in cost-related variables that best reflect the technical and programmatic conditions that define the scenario.

For sensitivity analysis, we know how large a cost difference is generated from different values for the input variables, but we do not necessarily know what technical and/or programmatic conditions are reflected in the cost sensitivity measure. So, while sensitivity analysis offers the ability to examine robustness of the estimate through arbitrary variances of the cost-related variables, there is no direct traceability back to specific technical and/or programmatic conditions that would bring about changes in cost. With the SBM, cost risk is directly characterized by virtue of having defined changes in technical and programmatic assumptions, not necessarily cost-related variables. So, although the SBM derives from sensitivity analysis, the SBM offers a direct characterization of the cost risks, whereas sensitivity analysis offers indirect characterization.

In this appendix, we describe the application of the SBM to a three-point communications approach (three-point communications approach for cost uncertainty analysis has been described in Chapter Six).[2] Applying the SBM to the three-point approach involves defining three scenarios and evaluating their respective costs. We term these three scenarios and their corresponding costs "anticipated," "optimistic," and "pessimistic." The anticipated scenario is the set of

---

[2] The original formulation of the SBM was based on the estimates for two scenarios: the "baseline" and "prime." The difference between the two was a measure of the risk reserve required to guard against the additional risks in the prime scenario. In the approach we outline in this appendix, we will modify the SBM to be consistent with the three-point communications approach. The major change is to define an additional scenario (the optimistic one).

technical and programmatic conditions that are expected during execution of the program—in other words, the baseline or point estimate (or also termed the baseline estimate in the original SBM formulation). The optimistic scenario identifies and incorporates additional opportunities for cost savings relative to the anticipated scenario and results in a lower cost. The pessimistic scenario identifies and incorporates select, additional risks relative to the anticipated scenario (which corresponds to the "prime" scenario in the original SBM). Figure F.1 shows the relationships of the scenarios for the three-point approach.[3]

Figure F.1
SBM Applied to a Three-Point Communications Approach

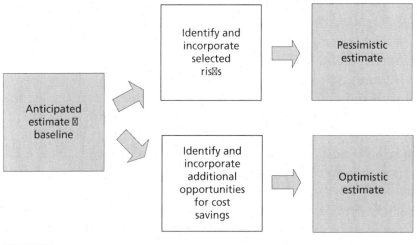

RAND *MG415-⊠1*

---

[3] It should be noted that the cost differences between the baseline and optimistic and pessimistic scenarios are not necessarily equal.

Generating Scenarios

Defining an Anticipated Scenario

The anticipated, or baseline, scenario is the set of technical and programmatic conditions that are expected during the course of completing the undertaking. Although these conditions should already be defined as part of generating the baseline costs estimate, we will review several pertinent issues. The cost analyst typically begins by reviewing the Cost Analysis Requirements Document (CARD).[4] The CARD officially documents the technical and programmatic information pertinent to the system acquisition. Careful review of the CARD will reveal what is to be acquired, the strategy and timeline for the acquisition, and assumptions and/or expectations about the environment in which the acquisition will occur. The CARD will generally provide the information required for the cost analyst to define the anticipated scenario. In some instances, the cost analyst will need to seek additional information from management personnel, the technical staff, and experts to clarify intent and expectations.

For the anticipated scenario, the cost analyst should strive for a set of technical and programmatic conditions that describe as normal a course of execution as possible. Consultations with the technical team, management personnel, and experts may help clarify what the expected conditions are. Integrating those consultations with information from the CARD can help the cost analyst formulate questions about areas that appear out of the norm or inconsistent. Refinements resulting from the questions will help the cost analyst identify what conditions are expected to be encountered and therefore should be part of the anticipated scenario.

The anticipated scenario should reflect the system descriptions available to the cost analyst. However, there may be circumstances in which the analyst might need to make more-conservative assumptions. For example, if the Technology Development Strategy[5] speci-

---

[4] See U.S. Department of Defense (1992) for details on the CARD.

[5] The Technology Development Strategy is developed during the Concept Refinement phase of a system acquisition. An approved Technology Development Strategy is a criterion

fies particularly ambitious goals, that ambitious outlook should be questioned and possibly altered in the technical and programmatic conditions set forth in the anticipated scenario. In defining an anticipated scenario, the cost analyst attempts to create a balanced picture of what is expected to occur, but he or she should not assume conditions contrary to information contained in official documentation without first questioning appropriate team members on the intent of goals and conditions that appear to diverge from more typical assumptions. Several iterations may be required to ensure that the anticipated scenario does not assume overly optimistic events, such as quick attainment of hoped-for technological breakthroughs, and also does not assume pessimistic circumstances, such as protracted subsystem solicitations.

Defining the Optimistic Scenario

The optimistic scenario is one that incorporates selected opportunities for further cost savings. The cost analyst examines the anticipated scenario and identifies *potential* opportunities for additional cost savings. For example, a hoped-for technical advance accomplished ahead of the planned schedule may be a potential cost savings opportunity. Or a material or production process improvement that might lead to a lower manufacturing cost could reduce the cost relative to the anticipated scenario.

Once the additional cost savings opportunities have been identified, the cost analyst designates a subset of these opportunities that are more likely to occur. Consultations with the technical and managerial staff can help with this process. This subset savings are then incorporated with the assumptions for the anticipated scenario. These changes modify some of the technical and programmatic conditions that define the anticipated scenario. This new scenario is called the optimistic scenario.

---

for attaining Milestone A and entering the Technology Development phase. See DoD Instruction 5000.2.

Defining the Pessimistic Scenario

A pessimistic scenario incorporates selected risks beyond those included in the anticipated scenario. The cost analyst begins by examining the anticipated scenario and identifying a set of events or circumstances that the technical staff or management team may want to guard against. The set of risks should be events or circumstances that might be expected to occur and will cause the cost of the undertaking to exceed the anticipated scenario cost. That is, the set of risks should not be the most extreme worst-case conditions, but rather, the set of conditions that the management team would want to have budget funds to guard against should any or all of the risks occur. The cost analyst can identify multiple risks and then choose a subset consisting of the most realistic and more likely to occur and/or those to guard against. Again, consultations with the technical staff and management team may help to identify which risks are viewed as most critical. Next, the cost analyst incorporates the chosen subset of risks into the anticipated scenario. The resulting new technical and programmatic conditions define a new scenario called the pessimistic scenario.

The Cost Uncertainty Analysis Resulting from the SBM Using Three-Point Scenarios

After defining and costing each scenario, the cost analyst will have a baseline cost estimate that corresponds to the anticipated scenario. In addition, the cost analyst will have a lower estimate corresponding to the optimistic scenario and a higher estimate corresponding to the pessimistic scenario. For all three cases, the cost analyst will be able to state exactly what technical and programmatic conditions occur that result in a specific cost. In the original SBM, the difference between the pessimistic estimate and the anticipated estimate defines the risk reserve.

Optional Statistical Augmentation of the SBM

The SBM generates a valid measure of cost risk; however, it does not generate confidence intervals. That is, the cost analyst does not have a measure of the probability that actual cost will be greater or less than a certain value. In the original formulation, Garvey (2005) set out a statistical augmentation to the SBM to define confidence intervals. As before, we will adapt the original formulation to the three-point approach.

The augmentation incorporates a statistical treatment based on the interval bounded by the optimistic and pessimistic estimates. The interval [Optimistic, Pessimistic] is of interest because it represents where the costs are reasonably expected to fall. Two assumptions must be made to define confidence intervals using this augmentation:

Assumption 1: Let α be the probability the actual cost of the system will fall in the interval [Optimistic, Pessimistic]. The cost analyst must specify a value for α. For example, one possible value for α would be 60 percent. This value is the first assumption.

Assumption 2: The second assumption is that the statistical distribution is uniformly distributed with probability α that the actual cost falls in the interval [Optimistic, Pessimistic].

Within these assumptions, the distribution of the total probability across the interval $[a, b]$ can be defined where b is the maximum cost of the system and a is the minimum cost of the system. The amounts a and b can be calculated from the known Optimistic and Pessimistic estimates and the value for α based on the equations below:

a_1 = Optimistic cost estimate
b_1 = Pessimistic cost estimate
α = Probability the actual cost is in the interval $[a_1, b_1]$

$$a = a_1 - (b_1 - a_1)\frac{(1-\alpha)}{2\alpha} \qquad \text{(F.1)}$$

$$b = b_1 - (b_1 - a_1)\frac{(1-\alpha)}{2\alpha} \qquad (F.2)$$

A percentile can be calculated with Equation F.3 (the probability that the system cost, *Cost*, will be at or below a certain value, *x*):

$$\text{Prob}(Cost \le x) = \frac{(x-a)}{(b-a)} \qquad (F.3)$$

With the following summary statistics:

$$Mean(Cost) = Median(Cost) = \frac{(a_1 + b_1)}{2} = \frac{(a+b)}{2} \qquad (F.4)$$

$$\text{ariance}(Cost) \equiv \sigma^2 = \frac{(b-a)^2}{12} = \frac{1}{12}\frac{(b_1 - a_1)^2}{\alpha^2} \qquad (F.5)$$

In Chapter Four, we used an example of the SBM in which there was a desire to guard against the risk of a 5 percent growth in weight and speed based on historical understanding of weight growth over a program and the concern that a new threat might change requirements. The total cost for the anticipated scenario was $2.9 billion and the pessimistic scenario was $3.0 billion. The optimistic scenario (one in which the weight is 5 percent lower than anticipated) corresponds to a cost of $2.8 billion. We have now defined the three-point ranges for the uncertainty analysis. If we assume that $\alpha = 0.6$, then $a = \$2.7$ billion and $b = 3.1$. The mean/median cost is $2.9 billion (which is the same as the anticipated cost for this example).

Designation of Selected Acquisition Report Milestones

To keep consistency across different changes to the acquisition systems and potential rebaselining of a program, the RAND Corporation has developed the following milestone definitions. Contract award dates are the primary determinative event to designate the dates of milestone baselines. When applying the following rules, keep in mind that the overall goal of milestone baseline determination is consistency of the estimate designation date with the date that the government commits to spending the funds for that program phase. For the most part, these definitions are generally consistent with the baselines published in the Selected Acquisition Reports (SARs).

The following rules apply to all system types except ships and submarines:

- The Milestone I (Dem/Val or equivalent) contract award date defines the Milestone I baseline. If no such effort is undertaken in the program—that is, the program begins with a full-scale development (FSD) or EMD contract award—then no Milestone I baseline is designated for the program.
- The Milestone II or IIA (FSD/EMD or equivalent) contract award date defines the Milestone II baseline. In the event that multiple developmental contracts are awarded in the program, the first contract of relatively significant value determines the Milestone II baseline date. The contract section of the SARs provides contract value information. If no such effort is undertaken in the program (i.e., the program begins with a produc-

tion contract award), then no Milestone II baseline is designated
for the program. This usually occurs if the program is a follow-
on procurement of an existing weapon system or if the program
is for the procurement of a substantially off-the-shelf product.

- The Milestone IIIA (low rate initial production [LRIP] or
equivalent) or Milestone III (full-rate production or equivalent)
contract award date defines the Milestone III baseline. Milestone IIIA is the preferred date for the Milestone III baseline,
but the actual commitment to production is defined by the relative magnitude of the value of the contract award, and the con-
tinuity of production stemming from that award date. If the
LRIP contract is of small relative value, and there is a break in
production following it before full-rate production is authorized,
then the Milestone III date is preferred for the Milestone III
baseline.

For ships and submarines:

- Milestone I and the Milestone I baseline are at the completion
of the baseline or preliminary design. Milestone II and the Milestone II baseline are at the award date for the lead ship's construction. Milestone III and the Milestone III baseline are at the
award date for the follow-on production contract or the exercise
of the first option for additional ships in the original contract.
Initial operational capability is the delivery of the lead ship, and
initial operational test and evaluation is indicated by the acceptance trials of the lead ship.

In the absence of milestones and contract award dates in a program, acquisition program baselines or other official baselines identified in the SAR can be used as the databases' baseline(s). The program's annual expenditures track, as well as the name given to the
baseline in the SAR, should be analyzed to determine whether a baseline represents Milestone I, II, or III.

In the absence of development funding, no Milestone I or II is
designated for the program.

Bibliography

Ames, B. N., R. Magaw, and L. S. Gold, "Ranking Possible Carcinogenic Hazards," *Science,* Vol. 236, 1987, pp. 271–280.

Anderson, Timothy P., "NRO Cost Group Risk Process," presentation for Space Systems Cost Analysis Group, July 16–17, 2003.

Augustine, Norman R., "RDT&E Cost Realism: Future Development Programs," memorandum for the Director of the Army Staff, July 12, 1974.

Bearden, David A., "Small Satellite Costs," *Crosslink* [Aerospace Corporation], Winter 2001, pp. 33–43. Online at www.aero.org/publications/crosslink/winter2001/ (as of September 2005).

Bedford, Tim, and Roger Cooke, *Probabilistic Risk Analysis: Foundations and Methods*, Cambridge, UK: Cambridge University Press, 2001.

Bentkover, Judith D., Vincent T. Covello, and Jeryl Mumpower, *Benefits Assessment: The State of the Art*, Dordrecht, The Netherlands: D. Reidel Publishing Company, 1986.

Berger, James O., *Statistical Decision Theory: Foundations, Concepts, and Methods*, Berlin: Springer-Verlag, 1980.

Bernstein, Peter L., *Against the Gods: The Remarkable Story of Risk*, New York: John Wiley & Sons, 1998.

Bevington, Philip R., and D. Keith Robinson, *Data Reduction and Error Analysis for the Physical Sciences*, New York: McGraw-Hill, 1969.

Book, Stephen A., "Justifying 'Management Reserve' Requests by Allocating 'Risk Dollars' Among Project Elements," Aerospace Corporation, Fall 1996 Meeting of the Institute for Operations Research and Management Science (INFORMS), Atlanta, Ga., November 3–6, 1996.

————, "Why Correlation Matters in Cost Estimating," DoD Cost Analysis Symposium, Williamsburg, Va., February 2–5, 1999.

————, "Estimating Probable System Cost," *Crosslink* [Aerospace Corporation], Vol. 2, No. 1, Winter 2001, pp. 12–21. Online at www.aero.org/publications/crosslink/winter2001/ (as of November 2005).

————, "Schedule Risk Analysis: Why It Is Important and How to Do It," SCEA National Training Conference and Educational Workshop, Phoenix, Ariz., June 11–14, 2002.

Book, Stephen A., and Philip H. Young, "General-Error Regression for Deriving Cost-Estimating Relationships," *Journal of Cost Analysis*, Fall 1997, pp. 1–28.

Bratvold, R., S. H. Begg, and J. C. Campbell, "Would You Know a Good Decision If You Saw One?" Society of Petroleum Engineers, SPE 77509, 2002.

Coleman, R. L., J. R. Summerville, and S. S. Gupta, "Considerations in Cost Risk Analysis: How the IC CAIG Handles Risk," Society of Cost Estimating and Analysis 2002 National Conference, 2002.

Connelly, Nancy A., and Barbara A. Knuth, "Evaluating Risk Communication: Examining Target Audience Perceptions About Four Presentation Formats for Fish Consumption Health Advisory Information," *Risk Analysis*, Vol. 18, No. 5, October 1998, pp. 649–659.

Conrow, Edmund H., *Effective Risk Management: Some Keys to Success*, Reston, Va.: American Institute of Aeronautics and Astronautics, 2000.

Cooper, Dale, and Chris Chapman, *Risk Analysis for Large Projects: Models, Methods, and Cases*, Chichester, N.Y.: John Wiley, 1987.

Coopersmith, Ellen, Graham Dean, Jason McVean, and Erling Storaune, "Making Decisions in the Oil and Gas Industry," *Oilfield Review*, Winter 2000/2001, pp. 2–9.

Defense Acquisition University, *AT&L Knowledge Sharing System CD*, Version 1.0a, April 2003a.

————, *Risk Management Guide for DOD Acquisition*, 5th ed., Version 2.0, June 2003b.

DeGroot, Morris H., *Optimal Statistical Decisions*, New York: McGraw-Hill, 1970.

DeMarco, Tom, *Controlling Software Projects: Management, Measurement, and Estimation*, New York: Yourdon Press, 1982.

Diekemann, James E., and W. David Featherman, "Assessing Cost Uncertainty: Lessons from Environmental Restoration Projects," *Journal of Construction Engineering and Management*, November/December 1998, pp. 445–451.

Diekemann, James, David Featherman, Rhett Moody, Keith Molenaar, and Maria Rodriguez-Guy, "Project Cost Analysis Using Influence Diagrams," *Project Management Journal*, December 1996, pp. 23–30.

Dienemann, Paul F., *Estimating Cost Uncertainty Using Monte Carlo Techniques*, Santa Monica, Calif.: RAND Corporation, RM-4854-PR, 1966.

Drezner, Jeffrey A., Jeanne M. Jarvaise, Ronald W. Hess, Paul G. Hough, and Dan Norton, *An Analysis of Weapon System Cost Growth*, Santa Monica, Calif.: RAND Corporation, MR-291-AF, 1993.

Driessnack, John, Noel Dickover, and Marie Smith, "Risk Community Building Inside the Program Management Community of Practice (PM COP)," *Acquisition Review Quarterly* [Defense Acquisition University], Spring 2003, pp. 107–114.

Eagleson, G. K., and H. G. Muller, "Transformations for Smooth Regression Models with Multiplicative Errors," *Journal of the Royal Statistical Society: Series B*, Vol. 59, No. 1, 1997, pp. 173–189.

Edwards, Ward, "Comment," on R. M. Hogarth, "Cognitive Processes and the Assessment of Subjective Probability Distributions," *Journal of the American Statistical Association*, Vol. 70, No. 350, 1975, pp. 291–293.

Einhorn, H. J., and R. M. Hogarth, "Ambiguity and Uncertainty in Probabilistic Inference," *Psychological Review*, Vol. 92, No. 4, 1985, pp. 433–461.

Ellsberg, D., "Risk, Ambiguity and the Savage Axioms," *Quarterly Journal of Economics*, Vol. 75, 1961, pp. 643–669.

Environmental Protection Agency, *Guidelines for Preparing Economic Analyses*, Office of the Administrator, EPA 240-R-00-003, 2000.

Fisher, Gene Harvey, *Cost Considerations in Policy Analysis*, Santa Monica, Calif.: RAND Corporation, P-5534, 1975.

Fisher, Gene Harvey, "The Problem of Uncertainty in Cost Analysis of Military Systems and Force Structures," unpublished RAND Corporation research, 1961.

———, *A Discussion of Uncertainty in Cost Analysis: A Lecture for the AFSC Analysis Course*, Santa Monica, Calif.: RAND Corporation, RM-3071-PR, 1962.

Fox, C. R., and A. Tversky, "Ambiguity Aversion and Comparative Ignorance," *Quarterly Journal of Economics*, Vol. 110, 1995, pp. 585–603.

Freeman, A. M., III, *The Benefits of Environmental Improvement*, Washington, D.C.: Resources for the Future, 1979.

Friel, John, Noreen Clancy, David Hutchison, and Jerry Sollinger, "Some Initial Thoughts on a Reserve Strategy for NASA's Office of Aerospace Technology," unpublished RAND Corporation research, December 2002.

Galway, Lionel A., "Quantitative Risk Analysis for Project Management: A Critical Review," RAND Corporation, WR-112-RC, 2004.

Garthwaite, Paul H., Joseph B. Kadane, and Anthony O'Hagan, *Elicitation*, Pittsburgh, Pa.: Carnegie Mellon University, Department of Statistics, Technical Report 808, 2004.

Garvey, Paul R., *Probability Methods for Cost Uncertainty Analysis*, Marcel Dekker, 2000.

———, "Cost Risk Analysis Without Statistics!!" 38th Department of Defense Cost Analysis Symposium, February 16, 2005.

Gatson, N., and P. Daniels, "Guidelines: Writing for Adults with Limited Reading Skills," U.S. Department of Agriculture, Food and Nutrition Service, 1988.

Henrici, Peter, *Elements of Numerical Analysis*, New York: John Wiley, 1964.

Hess, Ronald W., and H. P. Romanoff, *Aircraft Airframe Cost Estimating Relationships: Study Approach and Conclusions*, Santa Monica, Calif.: RAND Corporation, R-3255-AF, 1987.

Hillson, David, "Project Risk Management: Future Developments," *International Journal of Project and Business Risk Management*, Vol. 2, No. 2, 1998.

Hough, Paul G., *Pitfalls in Calculating Cost Growth from Selected Acquisition Reports*, Santa Monica, Calif.: RAND Corporation, N-3136-AF, 1992.

Howard, Truman, *Methodology for Developing Total Risk Assessing Cost Estimate (TRACE)*, Fort Lee, Va.: United States Army Logistics Management Center, November 8, 1978.

Jarvaise, Jeanne M., Jeffrey A. Drezner, and Dan Norton, *The Defense System Cost Performance Database: Cost Growth Analysis Using Selected Acquisition Reports*, Santa Monica, Calif.: RAND Corporation, MR-625-OSD, 1996.

Jarvis, Will, "Risk in Cost Estimating," briefing by OSD/PA&E, given at DoD Cost Analysis Symposium, Williamsburg, Va., January 29–February 1, 2002.

Johnson, Norman, and Samuel Kotz, *Continuous Univariate Distributions—1*, New York: Houghton-Mifflin, 1970.

Kadane, Joseph B., and Lara J. Wolfson, "Experiences in Elicitation," *The Statistician*, Vol. 47, No. 1, 1998, pp. 3–19 (with discussion).

Kahneman, Daniel, Paul Slovic, and Amos Tversky, *Judgment Under Uncertainty: Heuristics and Biases*, Cambridge, UK: Cambridge University Press, 1982.

Kelman, S., "Cost-Benefit Analysis: An Ethical Critique," *Regulation*, Vol. 5, No. 1, 1981, pp. 33–40.

Kitchenham, Barbara, Shari Lawrence Pfleeger, Beth McColl, and Sue Eagan, "A Case Study of Maintenance Estimation Accuracy," *Journal of Systems and Software*, Vol. 64, November 2002.

Klementowski, Lawrence J., *PERT/CPM and Supplementary Analytical Techniques: An Analysis of Aerospace Usage*, master's thesis, Wright-Patterson Air Force Base, Ohio: Air Force Institute of Technology, AFIT/GSM/SM/78S-11, 1978.

Klein, Gary, *Sources of Power: How People Make Decisions*, Cambridge, Mass.: MIT Press, 1998.

Korb, Kevin B., and Ann E. Nicholson, *Bayesian Artificial Intelligence*, London: Chapman & Hall/CRC, 2004.

Kuhn, K., and D. V. Budescu, "The Relative Importance of Probability, Outcomes and Vagueness in Hazard Risk Decisions," *Organizational Behavior and Human Decision Processes*, Vol. 68, 1996, pp. 301–317.

Lee, David A., *The Cost Analyst's Companion*, McLean, Va.: Logistics Management Institute, 1997.

Lovallo, D., and D. Kahneman, "Delusions of Success: How Optimism Undermines Executives' Decisions," *Harvard Business Review*, July 2003.

Markowitz, Harry, "Portfolio Selection," *Journal of Finance*, Vol. 7, No. 1 March 1952, pp. 77–91

Markowitz, Harry M., "The Early History of Portfolio Theory: 1600–1960," *Financial Analysts Journal*, July/August 1999, pp. 5–16.

Marshall, A. W., and W. H. Meckling, *Predictability of the Costs, Time, and Success of Development*, Santa Monica, Calif.: RAND Corporation, P-1821, 1959.

Massey, H. G., *Cost, Benefit, and Risk: Keys to Evaluation of Policy Alternatives*, Santa Monica, Calif.: RAND Corporation, P-5197, 1974.

Mayo, Deborah G., and Rachel Hollander, eds., *Acceptable Evidence: Science and Values in Risk Management*, New York: Oxford University Press, 1991.

Merrow, Edward W., Kenneth E. Philips, and Christopher W. Myers, *Understanding Cost Growth and Performance Shortfalls in Pioneer Process Plants*, Santa Monica, Calif.: RAND Corporation, R-2569-DOE, 1981.

McNicol, D. L., "Growth in the Costs of Major Weapon Procurement Programs," Institute for Defense Analyses, IDA Paper P-3832, 2004.

McNeil, B. J., S. G. Pauker, H. G. Sox, Jr., and A. Tversky, "On the Elicitation of Preferences for Alternative Therapies," *New England Journal of Medicine*, Vol. 306, 1982, pp. 1259–1262.

Morgan, M. Granger, "Choosing and Managing Technology-Induced Risk," *IEEE Spectrum*, Vol. 18, No. 12, 1981, pp. 53–60.

Morgan, M. Granger, and Max Henrion, *Uncertainty: A Guide to Dealing with Uncertainty in Quantitative Risk and Policy Analysis*, New York: Cambridge University Press, 1990.

Morgan, M. Granger, Baruch Fischhoff, Ann Bostrom, and Cynthia J. Atman, *Risk Communication: A Mental Models Approach*, New York: Cambridge University Press, 2002.

Morris, Peter W.G., *The Management of Projects*, London: Thomas Telford, 1994.

Mullin, Theresa M., *Understanding and Supporting the Process of Probabilistic Estimation*, doctoral thesis, Carnegie Mellon University, School of Urban and Public Affairs, 1986.

National Research Council, *Risk Assessment in the Federal Government: Managing the Process*, Washington, D.C.: National Academy Press, 1983.

———, *Improving Risk Communication*, Washington, D.C.: National Academy Press, 1989.

———, *Science and Judgment in Risk Assessment*, Washington, D.C.: National Academy Press, 1994.

———, *Understanding Risk: Informing Decisions in a Democratic Society*, Washington, D.C.: National Academy Press, 1996.

———, *Toward Environmental Justice: Research, Education, and Health Policy Needs*, Washington, D.C.: National Academy Press, 1999.

Novick, David, and Fredrick S. Pardee, *Reducing Lead-Time Through Improved Technological Forecasting: Some Specific Suggestions for More Usefully Formulated Projections of Technological Availability*, Santa Monica, Calif.: RAND Corporation, P-4122, 1969.

Ofek, Eli, and Matthew Richardson, "DotCom Mania: The Rise and Fall of Internet Stock Prices," *Stern Business*, Spring/Summer 2002.

O'Hagan, Anthony, "Eliciting Expert Beliefs in Substantial Practical Applications," *The Statistician*, Vol. 47, No. 1, 1998, pp. 21–35 (with discussion).

Pannell, Bobby J., *A Quantitative Analysis of Factors Affecting Weapons System Cost Growth*, master's thesis, Naval Postgraduate School, 1994.

Peeters, David, and George Dewey, "Reducing Bias in Software Project Estimates," *CrossTalk* [Journal of Defense Software Engineering], Vol. 13, No. 4, April, 2000, pp. 20–24.

Perry, Robert, Giles K. Smith, Alvin J. Harman, and Susan Henrichsen, *System Acquisition Strategies*, Santa Monica, Calif.: RAND Corporation, R-0733-PR/ARPA, 1971.

Pfleeger, Shari Lawrence, *Software Engineering: Theory and Practice*, 2nd ed., Upper Saddle River, N.J.: Prentice Hall, 2001.

Pfleeger, Shari Lawrence, Martin Shepperd, and Roseanne Tesoriero, *Decisions and Delphi: The Dynamics of Group Estimation*, Bournemouth, UK: Bournemouth University, May 2000.

Pfleeger, Shari Lawrence, Felicia Wu, and Rosalind Lewis, *Software Cost Estimation and Sizing Methods, Issues, and Guidelines*, Santa Monica, Calif.: RAND Corporation, MG-269-AF, 2005.

Plough, Alonzo, and Sheldon Krimsky, "The Emergence of Risk Communication Studies: Social and Political Context," *Science, Technology, & Human Values*, Vol. 12, Nos. 3–4, 1987, pp. 4–10.

Rasmussen, N. C., "The Application of Probabilistic Risk Assessment Techniques to Energy Technologies," *Annual Review of Energy*, Vol. 6, 1981, pp. 123–138.

Raymond, Fred, "Quantify Risk to Manage Cost and Schedule," *Acquisition Review Quarterly*, Spring 1999, pp. 147–155.

Resetar, Susan A., J. Curt Rogers, and Ronald W. Hess, *Advanced Airframe Structural Materials: A Primer and Cost Estimating Methodology*, Santa Monica, Calif.: RAND Corporation, R-4016-AF, 1991.

Roberts, Barney, Clayton Smith, and David Frost, "Risk-Based Decision Support Techniques for Programs and Projects," *Acquisition Review Quarterly* [Defense Acquisition University], Spring 2003, pp. 157–175.

Rodricks, Joseph V., and Michael R. Taylor, "Application of Risk Assessment to Food Safety Decision Making," *Regulatory Toxicology and Pharmacology*, Vol. 3, 1983, pp. 275–307.

Rooney, James J., and Lee N. Vanden Heuvel, "Root Cause Analysis for Beginners," *Quality Progress*, July 2004, pp. 45–53.

Roy, A. D., "Safety First and the Holding of Assets," *Econometrica*, Vol. 20, No. 3, July 1952, pp. 431–449.

Ruckelshaus, William D., "Risk, Science, and Democracy," *Issues in Science and Technology*, Vol. 1, No. 3, 1985, pp. 19–38.

Sapolsky, Harvey M., *The Polaris System Development: Bureaucratic and Programmatic Success in Government*, Cambridge, Mass.: Harvard University Press, 1972.

Schank, John F., Mark V. Arena, Denis Rushworth, John Birkler, and James Chiesa, *Refueling and Complex Overhaul of the USS Nimitz (CVN*

68): Lessons for the Future, Santa Monica, Calif.: RAND Corporation, MR-1632-NAVY, 2002.

Shepherd, Bill, "Managing Risk in a Program Office Environment," *Acquisition Review Quarterly* [Defense Acquisition University], Spring 2003, pp. 124–139.

Simon, Herbert, *Models of Bounded Rationality, Vol. I, II*, Cambridge, Mass.: MIT Press, 1982.

Slovic, Paul, "Informing and Educating the Public About Risk," *Risk Analysis*, Vol. 6, No. 4, 1986, pp. 403–415 [reprinted in Paul Slovic, *The Perception of Risk*, Earthscan, 2002].

Slovic, P., B. Fischhoff, and S. Lichtenstein, "Rating the Risks," *Environment*, Vol. 21, No. 3, 1979, pp. 14–20.

Small, M. J., B. Fischhoff, E. A. Casman, C. Palmgren, and F. Wu, *Protocol for Cryptosporidium Risk Communication*, Denver, Colo.: American Water Works Association Research Foundation, 2002.

Sobel, Steven, *A Computerized Technique to Express Uncertainty in Advanced System Cost Estimates*, Bedford, Mass.: MITRE, ESD-TR-65-79, 1965.

Solomon, Kenneth A., Pamela F. Nelson, and William E. Kastenberg, *Dealing with Uncertainty Arising Out of Probabilistic Risk Assessment*, Santa Monica, Calif.: RAND Corporation, R-3045-ORNL, 1983.

Tinker, T. L., and P. G. Silberberg, "An Evaluation Primer on Health Risk Communication Programs and Outcomes," Environmental Health Policy Committee, Subcommittee on Risk Communication and Education, U.S. Department of Health and Human Services, Public Health Services, 1997.

Tversky, A., and D. Kahneman, "Judgment Under Uncertainty: Heuristics and Biases," *Science*, Vol. 185, 1974, pp. 1124–1130.

———, "Rational Choice and the Framing of Decisions," *Journal of Business*, Vol. 59, 1986, pp. 251–278.

Tyson, K. W., B. R. Harmon, and D. M. Utech, "Understanding Cost and Schedule Growth in Acquisition Programs," Institute for Defense Analyses, IDA Paper P-2967, 1994.

U.S. Army, *Army Regulation AR 70-6*, June 16, 1986.

U.S. Department of Defense, *Department of Defense Cost Analysis and Guidance Procedures*, DoD 5000.4-M, December 1992

————, "Reprogramming of DOD Appropriated Funds," *DoD Financial Management Regulation*, Vol. 3, Ch. 6, August 2000.

————, *DoD Financial Management Regulation*, DoD 7000.14-R, Vol. 2A, June 2002.

U.S. Department of Defense Instruction Number 5000.2, *Operation of the Defense Acquisition System*, May 12, 2003.

Venzke, Gene A., *Implementation of Risk Assessment in the Total Risk Assessing Cost Estimate (TRACE)*, Carlisle Barracks, Pa.: U.S. Army War College, May 25, 1977.

Vose, David, *Risk Analysis: A Quantitative Guide*, New York: Wiley, 2000.

Wallenius, K. T., "Cost Uncertainty Assessment Methodology: A Critical Review," DoD Cost Analysis Symposium, 1985.

Wildavsky, Aaron, "No Risk Is the Highest Risk of All," *American Scientist*, Vol. 67, No. 1, 1979, pp. 32–37.

Williams, Terry W., *Modeling Complex Projects*, New York: Wiley, 2002.

Zerbe, Richard O., Jr., and Dwight D. Dively, *Benefit-Cost Analysis: In Theory and Practice*, New York: HarperCollins College Publishers, 1994.

Zsak, Mike, "DoD Risk Management," briefing by DoD Risk Working Group, May 5, 1997.